HOUSING AND
PUBLIC POLICY

An American Enterprise Institute Book

HOUSING AND PUBLIC POLICY
A Role for Mediating Structures

John J. Egan
John Carr
Andrew Mott
John Roos

BALLINGER PUBLISHING COMPANY
Cambridge, Massachusetts
A Subsidiary of Harper & Row, Publishers, Inc.

This book was written under the auspices of a project on mediating structures sponsored by the American Enterprise Institute, Washington, D.C., and funded, in part, by the Division of Education Programs of the National Endowment for the Humanities.

International Standard Book Number: 0-88410-827-9

Library of Congress Catalog Card Number: 80-20940

Printed in the United States of America

Library of Congress Cataloging in Publication Data
Main entry under title:

Housing and Public Policy

   "Written under the auspices of a project on mediating structures sponsored by the American Enterprise Institute."
   Includes index.
   1. Housing policy—United States. 2. Social institutions—United States. 3. Housing—Social aspects—United States. 4. Cities and towns—United States. I. Egan, John J. II. American Enterprise Institute for Public Policy Research.
HD7293.M358   363.5'8   80-20940
ISBN 0-88410-827-9

CONTENTS

FOREWORD

This volume on housing policies is an important part of a three year study of "mediating structures," directed by Peter Berger and myself and sponsored by the American Enterprise Institute. The controlling concept of the project, mediating structures, is not entirely new with us. Although called by different names, the concept is rooted in nineteenth and twentieth century social theory addressing the problems of modernity and, particularly, the role of the modern state in social change.

By mediating structures we mean those institutions that stand between the individual in his private life and the megastructures of society (big government, big labor, big corporations). The chief mediating structures are the family, the neighborhood, the church, and voluntary associations. Mediating structures may include other institutions, so long as they are "people sized" and have about them a face-to-face quality through which people can both feel and be empowered to control the decisions most crucial to their lives.

In advancing this concept and spelling out its policy implications, we hope to sustain the best of the policy approaches associated with the affirmative state, generally described as "New Deal." We believe, however, that the policies of the welfare state have been grievously, perhaps fatally, flawed by one key and fundamentally wrong assumption. That assumption is that public responsibilities must be exercised chiefly or exclusively through governmental action. We affirm a broad definition of public responsibilities. But we are convinced that most of those responsibilities can be more effectively, more economically, and more democratically exercised through the imaginative use of mediating structures. Justified complaints about "big government" are not directed so much at a comprehensive notion of what human needs should concern the government, but at the government's intrusion into people's lives by imposing its own ideas about how such needs should be met. Our premise is that in almost all instances the people most directly affected understand their needs best, and that public policies should be supportive of and ancillary to people's vision of their own good. Obviously, such vision is largely shaped by the values to which people subscribe. It is a primary strength of mediating structures that they are value-generating and value-bearing institutions. This is especially true of family, church, and voluntary associations.

The frequently well-intended policies of the welfare state have tended to undercut rather than to strengthen mediating structures. In the area of housing and elsewhere, the project involved a "minimalist" and a "maximalist" proposition. The minimalist proposition suggests that, wherever possible, public policies should be changed so they do not weaken mediating structures. The maximalist suggests that, wherever possible, public policies should be devised to utilize the strengths of mediating structures.

We are grateful to Monisgnor John Egan for accepting the chairmanship of the project's panel on housing. His recruitment and coordination of the team that produced this book are much appreciated. This volume is part of a series reflecting the work also of the four other panels—criminal justice, health, education, and welfare and child care. Under the controlling concept of mediating structures, each panel and each volume represents an effort to examine what public policies have been, how they have strengthened and weakened mediating structures, thus empowering or disempowering people, and to evaluate the merits of alternate policies proposed in both the past and present. Beyond that, it is hoped that each volume breaks new ground in exploring public policy designs that can enhance the freedom and well-being of our citizens.

This study on housing comes at a time when many observers believe that America is in political retreat from social problems in general and urban problems in particular. While the study encompasses many other aspects of housing, there is a special focus on urban housing and housing for the urban poor. The experience of Monsignor Egan and his associates has been, to a very large extent, in dealing with the problems of urban communities. Before accepting his present post at Notre Dame University, Monsignor Egan was for many years one of the chief actors on urban problems for the Roman Catholic Church in Chicago, the nation's largest archdiocese.

The mediating structures project and this part of it are offered in the confidence that ours need not be a time of fearful retreat and simple-minded retrenchment on social programs. Rather, it is a time to ask principal questions about the possibilities and limitations of government in a free society. It is a time to reconceptualize, and we are heartened that the mediating structures approach has been welcomed by policy planners on both the left and the right of the political spectrum. We believe ours is a time not so much for cutting back (although in some areas cutting back is clearly called for) as it is for cutting *through* the old liberal/conservative polarizations that too often have blinded us to what is actually happening in people's lives. Now and in the years immediately ahead, it appears that those who identify themselves as conservative will be in the policy-making saddle. Conservatism has too often been identified with negative reaction to the apparent mistakes and illusions of its opposition. But this can be an exciting time of testing whether conservatives have the nerve and imagination to advance the best in the humane intentions which liberals have claimed. The hope we propose is that the affirmative state need not be the oppressive state; that public policy is not a zero-sum game; that the prudent exercise of governmental power need not be at the price of disempowering those whom government is to serve.

Richard John Neuhaus
New York City

PREFACE

What follows should be read as an exploratory exercise and an incomplete one at that. About three years ago, we agreed to explore housing from the perspective of mediating structures. The concept of mediating structures, akin to many traditional social theories, such as subsidiarity, was elaborated in the work *To Empower People* by Peter Berger and Richard John Neuhaus.

Berger and Neuhaus, with the generous support of the American Enterprise Institute and the National Endowment for the Humanities, arranged for authors to test the viability of their concepts in the public policy arenas of housing, health, criminal justice, education, and welfare.

The book we have written has many shortcomings, some of which we are aware of. First, the book is not about all housing. It ignores many important areas, such as rural housing, mobile homes, and new trends in housing economics. We have simply selected some problems in housing to test the usefulness of the mediating structures concept in devising and implementing public policy.

The book omits or underemphasizes certain aspects of analysis. Little space is devoted to political theory and little space to large-scale quantitative analysis. The book is case oriented. One book cannot do everything, and we chose to illustrate the logic of the mediating structures approach through significant case studies.

The book has a particular time period in mind. It is directed toward policy makers considering the next five to eight years. One could usefully explore housing policy for the year 2000, but that would be another book.

The book's fourth shortcoming is the result of being written by four people. Although we shared basic outlooks, there were inevitably topics where the end product of our discussions was compromise rather than consensus. Although it resulted in large problems of coordination, perhaps this process more closely approximates the real world of policy formation.

The structure of the book is simple. Chapter 1 outlines the mediating structures concept as it relates to housing. Chapter 2 briefly examines the way public policy has affected mediating structures in the past. Chapters 3 through 6 take four problems in housing and examine the possible role of mediating structures in devising responses. The four areas are central city deterioration, "second tier" neighborhoods, suburban integration, and, finally, revitalization and gentrification—the process of private rehabilitation by predominantly white, affluent professionals from outside the neighborhood. Chapter 7 looks at some policy recommendations, and an epilogue examines some implications for mediating structures themselves.

There are many to whom we are grateful for assistance. First and foremost is Peggy Roach, without whose administrative and personal talents the project would never have been finished. Ted Kerrine, staff director for the project, was a source of constant support and assistance. Peter Berger and Richard Neuhaus, though not liable for our errors, provided invaluable critical readings of drafts.

Finally, we hope the book will be taken for what it is—a first step. We live in the hope that people's needs may be better served. May this work nourish that hope.

John J. Egan
John Carr
Andrew Mott
John Roos

1 INTRODUCTION

Since 1949 the United States has been committed by an act of Congress to the goal of "a decent house in a suitable living environment for every American family."[1] Thirty years after its enunciation, the goal remains elusive. Thirty years of slum clearance, urban renewal, public housing, Federal Housing Authority (FHA)-spurred suburban growth, and other measures have left the nation with large areas of severe housing need. This book attempts to examine that need, to articulate some of its causes, to examine past and present policies, and to investigate the usefulness of a mediating structures approach to housing policy.

HOUSING NEED

Few would argue that there are housing problems in America, but many disagree about the exact character of the problems. Some, for example, contend that having to spend more than 25 percent of income on housing is a form of deprivation. Others assert that inability to buy one's dream house in the suburbs is another form of deprivation and hence constitutes a housing need.

The authors are not unsympathetic to such concerns. But in general, we regard them as instances of desirable goals, with con-

1

siderably less urgency than the more compelling cases that we consider to be housing need. In our view, housing need should be defined primarily in terms of basic physical amenities and environmental decency at an affordable price. For example, some 6.3 million families live in housing without complete indoor plumbing or central heating or in buildings in extreme disrepair. Families in these circumstances have basic housing needs. But our concern, in keeping with following the goals of the 1949 Housing Act, is not limited to the simple physical structure of the house. Two other issues merit particular attention. In some cases, families are able to find structurally sound housing, but at the cost of spending such a large percentage of their incomes that such essentials as food and health are neglected. Others find decent structures, but in environments undesirable for anyone. Housing must be viewed not only as a structure at a price, but in the context of goods and services and environmental concerns. These include streets, schools, water and sewers, crime, and cleanliness.

There is no precise demarcation between basic needs and wants. But common sense indicates a great difference between the situation of a young couple trying to scrape together the down payment on an $80,000 house and the problem of a poor family living in a substandard structure in a crime-infested neighborhood. In general, our assumption is that public policy should concentrate on the greatest basic needs.

CAUSES

The causes of continued housing need are economic. This book, as stated in the preface, is not a systematic treatise on housing economics. But it does not proceed without certain general assumptions about causes of housing need. First, income plays a major role in allocating housing resources. Obviously, increased income and the elimination of racial and other barriers would significantly enhance the housing opportunities of some of those in greatest need. But a large-scale redistribution is unlikely in the short period we have chosen (five to eight years) and hence cannot be expected to play a major role in solving problems. Second, the fundamental patterns of central city decay continue to shape the prospects of many of our citizens. Any housing policy that does not consider these trends will miss much of the problem. The pattern is well known in its broad outlines. The nineteenth century and the first part of the twentieth century saw a massive trend toward urbanization. Beginning in the 1930s and accelerating after the Second World War, urban areas continued to grow, but central cities began to decline as a result of massive migrations of relatively affluent families to the suburbs. Inner city areas experienced grave decay. As residents attempted to flee, fragile second-tier neighborhoods began to falter and in many cases crumbled. Pressure then was put on suburban areas to provide both racial and class opportunity. The pattern is obvious in different degrees in all of our cities. One need only walk the streets not only of New York, Chicago, and Newark, but also of Dayton, South Bend, and San Antonio to see the ravages of blight and decay.

A third major assumption we make is that racism continues to plague American housing. We also assert that expectations about class continue to shape behavior in housing markets. Tragically, consumer attitudes continue mistakenly to intertwine the two, so that integration of a neighborhood tends to create fears that class change, accompanied by deteriorating property standards, will inevitably occur.

Fourth, we see the housing industry in America as primarily controlled by private megastructures such as the real estate industry, developers, mortgage bankers, builders, and insurance companies. Although government has some impact, the most important decisions about construction, financing, and insurance are made by large-scale for-profit institutions. Individuals and groups are relatively powerless to affect the policies of these megastructures.

Fifth, government policy has in many cases worsened rather than ameliorated these trends.

POLICY ALTERNATIVES

This is not a systematic book about causes of housing need, and it is not a systematic book about alternative solutions. The primary aim is to explore a housing policy based on the concept of mediating structures. In doing so, though, we must pay some attention to what the leading alternatives are for future public policy. We find three basic approaches: the pure market, the triage-dispersal strategy, and bureaucratic rebuilding. Following are a brief description and critique of each.

Pure Market

The pure market theory takes a long view and is rooted in classical economics. It argues that the market will respond to consumer demands and over the long run will allocate resources efficiently. Areas of blight and decay will eventually depopulate. At some point they will be priced attractively enough for revitalization by the private sector. If any government action should be taken, it should be in the form of pure income supplements, allowing poor people to compete more effectively in the marketplace. If neighborhoods cannot be sustained by economic forces, they should not be artificially "saved" by government intervention.

Our objection to this view centers on assumptions about the free market and on short-term and long-term effects. The free market analogy assumes a sensitive response by markets to consumer needs. In fact, we find markets dominated by megastructures that are insensitive to consumer needs, especially at lower income levels. Practices such as redlining, mortgage "churning," and blockbusting, discussed in later chapters, are too pervasive to allow much credibility for "the market" as problem solvers. The second disagreement with this stance concerns the time span. Admittedly, over the long run, market forces will probably redevelop even such blighted areas as the South Bronx. Our objection is that this may take twenty to thirty years. In the meantime hundreds of thousands of residents are subjected to the devastating experience of urban decay. As will be seen in Chapter 3, "Landlords of Last Resort," the process of disinvestment in such areas brings great human suffering.

Triage Dispersal

The South Bronx is a good case for the second basic alternative, triage dispersal. The position presented here is a composite abstraction of several views, but it represents one basic set of attitudes often found among planners and decision makers. According to this view, some areas are so bad that, to use the medical analogy,

they must be cordoned off and allowed to die, saving scarce resources for more viable neighborhoods.

It is often assumed that most poor neighborhoods are unable to
sustain a viable environment. Some argue that government should
intervene and disperse the poor population throughout the suburban
ring. Another variant argues that this will occur naturally, leaving
the city smaller but more vital.

Several objections occur to us. First, many residents of inner
city neighborhoods want to stay there. No one wants to stay in
the South Bronx with crime and arson rampant. But, as some of
our cases illustrate, substantial numbers of residents would, with
adequate assistance, choose to stay and rebuild their neighborhoods.
Second, the dispersal strategy to the suburbs is an illusion. There
has not been, nor will there be, significant forced integration across
municipal lines in the next ten years. Further, significant decentral-
izing migration patterns among the poor are a very long-term phenomenon. There are 800,000 people in the South Bronx, the vast
majority Spanish speaking. Immigrants, legal and illegal, continue
to arrive there from some twenty-nine countries. It is inconceivable
that in the short run they will choose or be able to move to Dubu-
que, Grand Rapids, or Chillicothe. Opportunities for choosing such
alternatives should be encouraged, but for the next ten years substantial numbers of people will remain in poor urban areas. If no
revitalization efforts are mounted, many residents will move, not
to the outer reaches of Long Island, but rather to the next weakest
neighborhood. The classic pattern is that this migration centers on
one or a few neighborhoods at a time, ultimately destabilizing them
and causing another ring of blight and decay to set in. Realistically,
to say that Chicago's poor South Side neighborhoods are unviable
and should be abandoned is to say that Marquette Park and other
nearby middle-income neighborhoods will be subject to a flood of
refugees and attendant immense and often irreversible pressures.

Bureaucratic Rebuilding

The third alternative is the classic bureaucratic one, which is to rebuild
areas through the actions of government. This was one major element
of urban renewal and public housing policies of the 1950s and 1960s.
Our objection, elaborated later, is that like private megastructures,

public megastructures usually fail to take into account the people they are designed to serve and often result in more harm than good.

MEDIATING STRUCTURES APPROACH

The approach, or hypothesis, that we will explore in this book, is based on the assumption that public policy should be redirected to take account of the role of mediating structures of family, neighborhood, voluntary associations, and church. At the very least, government should refrain from policies that damage these mediating structures. In the best case, government should actively involve mediating structures in the design and delivery of services.

Such a policy would take seriously the claim that people find meaning in those associations that stand as mediators between them as individuals and the impersonal megastructures, both public and private. It also recognizes that these associations can often determine and achieve the legitimate objectives of members better than impersonal bureaucracies. It agrees with the fundamental objectives of government welfare and housing policy, but it argues that these objectives can best be met by pursuing a policy that promotes rather than damages mediating structures.

At present, a housing policy based on mediating structures is in part hypothesis and needs investigation. But there are tentative arguments in its favor.

First, it works. We shall present evidence that in many cases mediating structures do a better job than public and private bureaucracies of meeting specific housing goals.

Second, the desire for shared meanings and understandings among voluntary groups of citizens is a real and substantial yearning. Given the liberal and procedural character of our society, room should be allowed for developing deeper bonds at levels lower than the state.

Third, within strict constitutional bounds, government policy should aim at enabling, or empowering, people to meet their own needs and achieve their own objectives. Mediating structures such as church and neighborhood groups are more responsive to these needs and objectives than private or public megastructures.

Fourth, political will at the national level depends on the satisfaction of the citizens. Citizens will not support policies that damage structures they hold dear, such as neighborhoods, church, and family. A mediating structures policy, respecting these institutions, can help reverse the present lack of commitment to adequate housing.

Fifth, the future of most urban neighborhoods depends on the way in which excruciating problems of human interaction are faced. In most cases, the demand for or the desirability of housing stock is determined more by the neighborhood environment than by the physical structure. Successful revitalization projects depend more on the effect they have on fragile and complex human relations than on physical construction. Mediating structures have significant advantages over public and private bureaucracies in dealing with these human problems.

Sixth, state action is often justified as being for the common good. Mediating structures are often viewed as detrimental to the larger good, being particular and local in character. We believe that mediating structures are not oblivious of the common good and can help to develop common principles of justice. As will be seen, we in no way belittle the need for national *public* decisions about rights and duties. Our claim is that within this framework, room exists for smaller experiments in developing shared meanings that benefit the wider society.

It is obvious that each of these tentative arguments can be turned around to be indictments. But it would be better in reading the balance of the book, if they were read as questions. For example: *Do* mediating structures perform well? *Do* they represent the needs and objectives of citizens better than markets or bureaucracies? *Is* it possible to establish constitutional and legal frameworks that ensure against illegitimate use of public funds for private ends, as too often happened in large urban renewal programs?

REFERENCE

1. Housing Act of 1949, preface.

2 HOUSING POLICY AND THE NEGLECT OF MEDIATING STRUCTURES

Since the 1930s, nineteen major pieces of federal legislation dealing with housing laws have been enacted. The government has sought to administer more than a dozen major housing programs. Billions of dollars have been spent, and thousands of regulations issued. Forty years of federal housing activity have led to almost universal disenchantment with the government's performance in meeting the needs of the American people. Conservatives point to wasted money; progressives speak of unmet needs and wasted opportunities. Those most directly affected by government policies are remarkably ambivalent about a given program's value and impact.

Developers and builders simultaneously blame inadequate funding and too much governmental intervention for the industry's inability to build sufficient housing. Community activists point to federal policies encouraging freeways and suburban sprawl as key contributors to urban neighborhoods' decline. Organizations of the poor point to the lack of federal commitment and a mistaken sense of priorities in explaining the failures of federal housing policies.

Perhaps the most serious problem of national housing policy is the way one decade's "solution," proposed with hope and confidence, seems to contribute, through flawed design and maladministration, to the next decade's problems. Consider the following examples:

- Urban renewal, the strategy of the 1950s, destroyed far more homes than it built.
- The St. Louis Housing Authority was forced to dynamite parts of the $36 million Pruite-Igoe high-rise public housing project less than twenty years after it was built. Ironically, Pruite-Igoe had won an American Institute of Architects award for design excellence.
- The FHA subsidy programs in the 1960s and early 1970s, designed to increase homeownership and combat slums, resulted in HUD's becoming the largest "slumlord" in many major cities.
- The Urban Policy, proclaimed by President Jimmy Carter, was designed to compensate for past federal policies that created incentives to abandon the cities. However, it was woefully inadequate and failed to receive congressional backing and sufficient funding.

There are, of course, more positive statistics and cases; "Substandard" housing declined from 50 percent in 1940 to 7 percent in the 1970s; successful renewal of downtown areas has occurred in San Francisco, Minneapolis, and other cities; remarkably good low-rise public housing across the country has provided decent housing for thousands of poor families; and government has assisted housing rehabilitation and neighborhood renewal that never could have happened without public support. But all too often, federal housing policy has done more harm than good, and federal housing programs have led to bitter disappointment.

Housing legislation has been influenced far more by the priorities of financial institutions, developers, and the real estate industry than by the needs of individual families and neighborhoods. Far more effort has been spent in designing financial mechanisms to ensure a financial return for bankers and builders than in designing housing in which families can live and prosper. Programs and processes of program planning are too often fashioned to meet the desires of planners and governmental officials without adequate consideration of the need to involve neighborhood residents and community organizations. These very real biases toward financial interests and elitist attitudes have contributed in a major way toward the repeated failures in housing policy.

Before turning to particulars, an overall assessment of U.S. housing policy might be fairly stated as follows: The first of the goals of the landmark 1949 Housing Act has been achieved with some success; only in recent years have we realized that the second goal is not being achieved and is both more difficult and more important. The two goals are found in the preface of the act: "A decent home and a suitable living environment for every American family." As stated, there is evidence of progress on the goal of a decent home. In 1940 about 50 percent of the nation's housing stock lacked complete plumbing or was otherwise deficient. In 1950 the figure was 36.9 percent; in 1960, 18.2 percent; and in 1970, 7 percent. Not even counting tax benefits, the federal government alone has spent more than $100 billion since 1934 on housing and urban development. With respect to gross physical condition, American housing was better in 1977 than in any previous period. At the same time, much evidence, both statistical and practical, pointed to a drastic failure of the second goal, that of a "suitable living environment."

Increasingly, the urban crisis is described not only in terms of leaking roofs or inadequate plumbing but also in the human, communal aspects of residence. Crime, fear, drugs, pollution, noise, alienation, loss of community, atrophied educational systems, inadequate services, social disruption more and more become the key words for discontent with American housing. Most would agree that the human and social environment of housing in America has been relatively unimproved by housing policy.

The following sections analyze some of the major government policies in housing. This is not a systematic history of government's involvement. The aim is to look at selected government policies from the perspective of mediating structures.

THE FEDERAL HOUSING ADMINISTRATION

The Federal Housing Administration was one of the earliest and most important federal initiatives in housing. Before the 1930s housing was primarily a private responsibility. Some local governments and local charitable institutions provided ad hoc assistance to destitute persons and the victims of fire and natural disasters, but there was no national housing policy or activity. In 1908 President Theodore Roosevelt appointed a presidential commission on housing, which recommended that the federal government condemn, purchase, and rehabilitate much of the nation's slum housing. The proposal went nowhere.

It took the depression of the 1930s to bring about federal involvement in the nation's housing problems. Some public housing was built by the federal government itself under Works Progress Administration (WPA) programs. Several of these well-constructed projects, now more than forty years old, still provide decent and safe housing for poor families. This unique venture in direct federal production of housing was halted by court order in 1935 over issues of eminent domain.

The National Housing Act of 1934 established the Federal Housing Administration, the dominant force in federal housing until the 1960s. One of the least controversial New Deal agencies, it has insured more than 11 million residential mortgages worth nearly $200 billion. Its major contribution to housing policy was the popularization of the long-term, low down payment, fully amortizing mortgage. Through the FHA programs of mortage insurance, more families in the 1940s and 1950s were able to become homeowners than in the previous 150 years. This phenomenal level of activity was a great boon to individual families seeking the privacy, independence, and enjoyment of their own suburban homes. Sixty percent of American families own their own houses today, many of them still making payments on FHA mortgages.

However, the consequences of FHA activity for cities were another matter. From the beginning FHA turned its back on cities and minority families to underwrite the mass movement of white middle-class families to the suburbs, a movement further abetted by government-supported highway construction. FHA model convenants and procedures helped to create racially segregated neighborhoods. FHA urged the use of restricted racial covenants until they were ruled unenforceable by the courts in 1948. Even after that FHA saw "homogeneous" neighborhoods as safeguards of its financial investment. It took President John F. Kennedy's executive order of November 1962 to prohibit racial segregation in FHA programs.

The results of early FHA discrimination are still with us today.

Black Americans are only half as likely to own their own homes as white Americans. Housing segregation, particularly in the FHA-financed suburbs, is far harder to combat than racial discrimination in employment, education, and public accommodations.

FHA's exclusive concentration on new construction ignored the need for rehabilitation and repair of older, still sound housing stock in inner urban areas. From 1934 to 1960, FHA provided significant incentives to abandon the cities for the greener pastures of suburbia.

During these years the FHA functioned as a large insurance agency guaranteeing market-rate loans to qualified families. In the 1960s this role changed sharply. FHA became a source of below-market interest loans, and its focus now included inner city areas. Ironically, the staid insurance agent of the white suburban exodus became the bankroller of the subsidy programs of the 1960s and 1970s—with scandalous results.

Various FHA subsidy programs (221 (d) 3, 235, 236) provided decent housing for large numbers of people. Nonprofit, community-based groups, such as local churches and community organizations, were able to use these programs to provide housing for low- and moderate-income families. The record of these efforts is mixed. In some cases nonprofit groups simply fronted for developers, and there was no qualitative difference between these community-based efforts and the projects of independent developers. In other cases, well-intentioned but inexperienced community groups were unable to provide adequate management and maintenance of the housing. Their projects fell into default or disrepair. In a significant number of cases, however, community-based development efforts provided better housing and environments for families. More sensitive management, an understanding of the community, greater involvement of tenants, and the provision of a range of social services marked these successful endeavors. Later chapters examine specific cases of successful and failed community-based housing development.

FHA subsidy programs also opened the door to speculation, outrageous profit, and exploitation. These programs were used extensively by blockbusters and shoddy builders to make enormous profits. Under one program (235), speculators bought dilapidated buildings cheap, provided a few cosmetic touches, and sold them for double or triple the purchase price.

These abuses led to more than 1,000 criminal indictments, suspension of the program, and thousands of abandonments. By the mid-1970s, the Department of Housing and Urban Development (HUD) owned more than 4,000 homes in Philadelphia and almost 25,000 units in Detroit. The House Banking Committee called the units "almost slums." One analyst called it "a deliberate program of urban ruin for profit under the cover of government housing law and an endless flow of federal money."[1] Great damage was done to neighborhoods by the abuse of FHA subsidy programs, so much that Robert Embrey, former commissioner of housing in Baltimore and later HUD assistant secretary, called FHA "the kiss of death" in urban rehabilitation.[2]

Under the FHA subsidy programs, financial returns were guaranteed for builders, banks, and real estate firms. But there was no guarantee of the quality of the housing for the new owners or tenants. Many units were substandard. Others were poorly constructed or poorly rehabilitated. These units were soon abandoned by low-income families, who could not afford the cost of maintenance and major repairs. The same agency that helped create the suburban communities in the forties, fifties, and sixties was now helping to destroy inner city communities, to the severe detriment of mediating structures.

URBAN RENEWAL

The Housing Act of 1949 also established the nation's second major housing strategy: an ambitious program of slum clearance. Urban renewal, as it came to be called in the 1950s, provided financial assistance of more than $10 billion, permitting local public housing authorities to condemn tracts of blighted land, clear them, and make them available to private developers. The program did eliminate some of the worst slums and provided a boost to downtown revitalization in several cities: San Francisco, Minneapolis, Boston, and Pittsburgh, among others. However, it also resulted in the disruption of the lives of an estimated one million people. In addition, it displaced an estimated 100,000 small business establishments and contributed to the demise of 35,000 of them. As a housing strategy, it was a bitter failure, destroying far more homes (425,000) than it built (125,000), and much of the replacement housing was far too expensive for the original residents. This led to more overcrowding and higher rents in low-income areas. Even when relocation

,ventually provided, families not only had to move but
 n from a supportive network of friends and associations
 kely could not be replaced.

 renewal placed enormous pressures on already precarious
 g communities, those least able to accommodate the influx
 r and dependent families. As Herbert Gans reported:

A 1961 study of renewal projects in 41 cities showed that 60% of the dis-
possessed tenants were merely located in other slums; and in big cities the
proportion was ever higher. Renewal sometimes even created new slums
by pushing relocatees into areas and buildings which then became over-
crowded and deteriorated rapidly.[3]

From a mediating structures perspective, urban renewal was seriously
flawed. Its approach to many neighborhoods was a variation on the
Vietnam theme: "We had to destroy the town in order to save it."
Particularly in the early years of the program, renewal efforts seemed
focused far more on abstract plans and downtown priorities than
neighborhood survival and affordable housing for families. Community opposition or involvement was often treated as an ob-
struction rather than a legitimate voice of restraint. Urban renewal
disrupted family and community ties without thought to the consequences for people and neighborhoods. It was an obvious mani-
festation of a strategy treating housing as a physical commodity
rather than a setting for family and community. The "urban prairies"
that still dot inner cities are a testimony to the failed vision and over-
confidence of the "experts" who gave us "Negro removal," as urban
renewal came to be called.

PUBLIC HOUSING

The third major strategy of national housing policy—public housing—
was first authorized by the Housing Act of 1947, the product of
a surprising coalition of liberal Democrats and "Mr. Republican,"
Senator Robert Taft of Ohio. Since 1947, more than one million
units have been constructed by 1,200 local housing agencies. Public
housing, despite controversy and serious mistakes is the only federal
housing program to serve large numbers of poor families.

Most contemporary observers would not recognize public housing
in its early years. The housing resulting from the 1947 act and the

Housing Act of 1949 consisted predominantly of low-rise, two- or three-story apartment buildings. They were for mostly young, employed working-class families. Jimmy and Rosalyn Carter were residents in public housing in Plains, Georgia, in the early years of their marriage.

Beginning in the mid-1950s, the tenants of new public housing changed sharply, as did the design. Higher urban land costs led to more and more high-rise buildings. Municipal housing authorities and elected officials decided to concentrate the buildings, isolating public housing residents. Large numbers of poor families crowded into the projects. Architectural designs took little account of the needs of families with children; high-rise buildings had fewer bedrooms and little recreational space or open area. In some instances, design standards were lowered to make public housing less attractive and force more reliance on the private sector. Public housing became more and more segregated. Before 1940 between one-fourth and one-third of public housing residents were black; currently 45 percent are black.

In some communities "the projects" became code words for poverty, crime, and despair. The concentration of poor families in massive high-rises was a tragic mistake—a "cure" far worse than the disease. It unfavorably affected schools and other institutions. Several studies found that high- or low-rise construction was a better indicator of crime in public housing than the percentage of welfare families.[4] Oscar Newman found in New York that the number of robberies was in direct proportion to the size of the building.[5] A Ford Foundation study in St. Louis showed that the rate of crime was 50 to 80 percent lower in a low-rise building than in a high-rise directly across the street.[6]

As public housing grew skyward, it became more and more unpopular in the broader community, leading to greater concentration of public housing in politically powerless neighborhoods that were least able to withstand the pressures. Finally, Congress outlawed high-rise construction and provided rental subsidies and incentives for better management in public housing.

In the last few years, public housing has been revived somewhat as communities attempt to meet the housing needs of poor families through the production of low-rise and scattered-site public housing.

The lessons seem clear: Ignoring the needs of families in the design, location and construction of housing is disastrous. Furthermore, the concentration of very large numbers of poor and dependent families can easily overwhelm management capabilities and the social and economic stability of the surrounding neighborhood.

THE DEPARTMENT OF HOUSING AND URBAN DEVELOPMENT

In the early 1960s, President Kennedy pushed without success for the establishment of a cabinet-level agency concerned with housing and cities. Finally, in September 1965, the Department of Housing and Urban Development was established to administer FHA programs, public housing, urban renewal, secondary mortgage markets, and a variety of other urban programs. Then a major expansion of federal housing activity was legislated even as the deep problems in urban renewal and public housing began to surface.

Perhaps the most innovative but disappointing program in the history of federal policy was the "Model Cities" program enacted in 1966. Although some local projects made a real difference for low- and moderate-income people, the program was accompanied by excessive rhetoric and expectations, rapid and unplanned growth, and widespread conflicts over political control.

Designed by a government task force, "Demonstration Cities" was designed to pour resources into a few communities in an effort to concentrate and coordinate federal programs, bring together and develop local leadership, provide settings for innovation, and encourage local initiative. "Demonstration Cities" became "Model Cities." A "few communities" became 50, then 100. And the funding for the program was reduced. Issues of citizen participation and political control were never really settled. "Turf" battles raged between "poverty" officials and representatives of local government.

In some ways, the Model Cities program is a lesson in how to coopt the idea of mediating structures without actually involving them. New community structures were often set up without any consideration of established neighborhood institutions or leaders. A new class of petty bureaucrats that ignored indigenous leadership arose.

In 1968 Congress passed legislation establishing new FHA subsidy programs and goals for the following decade of 26 million housing units (6 million of which were to be government subsidized). Under the leadership of Secretary George Romney of HUD, the Nixon administration achieved an unparalleled level of construction of subsidized housing. Before the 1968 act, construction had never exceeded 100,000 units per year. In 1970 some 400,000 units were started. Romney pushed the new programs hard and sought new technological breakthroughs in the design of low-cost housing. But in January 1973, HUD suspended all housing subsidy programs, model cities, and urban renewal because of excessive cost and scandals within the programs. The Nixon moratorium brought federal housing construction to a halt. Romney's production emphasis had been out of step with the Nixon policies of the "new federalism."

The administration undertook a major review of national housing policy. Some hundred persons labored for almost two years to bring forth *Housing in the Seventies,* an indictment of past subsidies on grounds of cost inequity and inefficiency. The study was widely regarded as an attempt to justify the dismantling of the housing subsidy programs and as a prelude to some form of the block grants and housing allowance approaches.

The Housing Act of 1974 was the result of the battle between the administration and Congress over the future of housing policy. It was a dramatic change from the categorical grant programs (urban renewal, model cities, water and sewer, and others) to a single block grant to cities and counties for community development. The grants were for eliminating blight, assisting low-income and middle-income neighborhoods, and "other priority needs." They were also designed to eliminate red tape and federal interference in local decisions. Block grants were characterized by opponents as a retreat from concern for the poor and as less money in a more politically palatable form.

Cities chose to spend their money on a wide variety of projects, ranging from housing rehabilitation to tennis courts in affluent neighborhoods, but it is clear that cities spent far less on low- and moderate-income neighborhoods than would have been required under the categorical programs.

In 1977 the program was reviewed by Congress. Different formulas were designed, assigning higher priority to older and more distressed cities and mandating greater attention to the needs of poor and moderate-income families. A special program of Urban Development Action Grants (UDAG) was added to assist cities in major economic development and rehabilitation efforts.

In addition the 1974 act, though not killing the earlier subsidy programs, placed primary emphasis on a new kind of leased housing program (Section 8). This program straddles the fence between a housing allowance and a subsidy to developers. It provides a contract with a landlord to pay the difference between the fair market rent of a unit and 20 percent of a poor tenant's income. Although it is not a construction or an interest subsidy for a builder or owner, it is also not a cash payment for the use of the tenant in obtaining housing.

REHABILITATION

In the late 1960s there was also a shift in national housing policy from a virtually exclusive preoccupation with new construction to a realization that conservation and rehabilitation of existing housing ought to be a major priority. By 1977 approximately one-third of the construction activity in the United States was in rehabilitation of homes.

Federal lawmakers made a serious mistake in neglecting so long the enormous investment in existing housing—approximately $1.5 trillion. Although the housing law has been changed to permit rehabilitation, the idea receives more lip service than government dollars. Earlier attempts to get federal support for rehabilitation could have been prophetic. In 1964 the Section 312 program was established, but funding was low, and the program ran into severe administrative problems. One study estimated that the cost of administering 312 was roughly equal to the total dollars provided for rehabilitation.

Once again the priorities of the home building, banking, and real estate industries seem to have overshadowed federal policy at the expense of the families, neighborhoods, and community groups seeking to preserve and renew communities and homes.

REDLINING

A major threat to housing and urban neighborhoods has been the process of disinvestment and redlining. The systematic withdrawal of mortgage money, home improvement loans, insurance coverage, and other services has left many neighborhoods without the resources to combat blight.

Despite a long history of government charter and regulation of financial institutions (going back to the Federal Home Loan Bank of 1932), it was not governmental policy or action that first sought to curb disinvestment. Rather, it was determined community groups that in the early 1970s researched the patterns of investment, confronted the financial institutions, obtained changes in lending policies, and worked for federal legislation. The Home Mortgage Disclosure Act of 1975, which requires federally chartered financial institutions to disclose their lending data to the public, was devised, lobbied, and passed as a result of the work of hundreds of community organizations across the country.

NEIGHBORHOOD HOUSING SERVICES

One of the more innovative and low-profile efforts of the federal government has been the Neighborhood Housing Services (NHS) program of the Urban Reinvestment Task Force. This cooperative effort of the Home Loan Bank Board, HUD, and other federal regulatory agencies is designed to encourage reinvestment in urban areas.

The typical NHS program, based on a Pittsburgh model, is a partnership of community residents, leaders of financial institutions, and representatives of local government. The lenders agree to make mortgage and home improvement loans to qualified borrowers in the target neighborhoods as well as to fund the costs of the NHS program. City officials commit themselves to improve services and guarantee a sensitive program of code enforcement. The program also includes a high-risk revolving loan fund to make loans at flexible rates to borrowers who cannot qualify for conventional financing.

The NHS is governed by a private, nonprofit board in each community. In each case, more than half of the decision makers are neighborhood residents. A small staff for administration and counseling usually costs around $30,000 to $50,000 annually. From the initial effort in Pittsburgh, NHS grew to include 25 cities by 1976 and expected 100 programs by 1980.

THE CARTER ADMINISTRATION

The Carter administration housing record cannot yet be assessed. Mr. Carter's first HUD secretary, Patricia Harris, who came to her job with no experience in housing, appointed Monsignor Geno Baroni, a national neighborhood spokesman, to the redefined position of assistant secretary for neighborhood, voluntary organizations, and consumer affairs. The administration arranged a new formula for the Community Development Block Grants program, designed to be more sensitive to older and more distressed cities. The administration proposed and had passed the Urban Development Action Grants program. President Carter supported and signed a bill establishing a National Committee on Neighborhoods.

His new urban policy, though giving greater recognition to neighborhoods and other mediating structures than previous pronouncements, did not initially seem to reflect a real commitment to assist and strengthen those structures. The urban policy was remarkably void of housing provisions—no new initiatives in rehabilitation or housing for poor or middle-income families.

CONCLUSION

What is needed is not more rhetoric about neighborhoods. In fact, we must avoid repackaging old ideas or wrapping a sociological term around the new interest in neighborhoods. We need to reverse the policies of the last forty years, policies that have been extraordinarily detrimental to mediating structures. To avoid the mistakes of the past, we need housing policies that maximize individual choice, give power to people and the institutions they value most, and demonstrate an understanding and respect for the value of genuine pluralism. This advocacy of mediating structures is not an argument for a reduction or abandonment of federal housing programs or funding. On the contrary, we believe even greater governmental housing assistance will probably be required to meet needs. However, the country needs a policy with new assumptions and approaches based on the recognition of the central roles mediating structures can play in meeting housing needs.

This brief and selective review of federal housing policy is not a total indictment of past efforts; it has emphasized specific weak points and failures. It does so not to suggest a comprehensive alternative, but rather to open discussion on ways in which a mediating structures perspective might significantly enhance public policy.

REFERENCES

1. Brian Boyer, *Cities Destroyed for Cash* (Chicago: Follett, 1973).
2. Robert Embrey, testimony before House Banking Committee (U.S. House of Representatives, September 22, 1976).
3. Herbert J. Gans, "The Failure of Urban Renewal," in Bellush and Hausknecht, eds., *Urban Renewal: People, Politics and Planning.* (Garden City, N.Y.: Doubleday Anchor, 1967), p. 467.
4. Martin Mayer, *The Builders* (New York: Norton, 1978), p. 191.
5. Oscar Newman, *Defensible Space* (New York: Macmillan, 1972), p. 193.
6. Quoted in Mayer, *The Builders,* p. 191.

3 LANDLORDS OF LAST RESORT

The South Bronx has become a vivid symbol of urban neglect. The very mention of the area brings frightening pictures to mind—abandonment, rubble, fire, and crime.

Even far north of the South Bronx, past Yankee Stadium, past the major hospitals, past the Grand Concourse and billions of dollars of investment in apartment buildings, the devastation continues. Block after block, once solid buildings stand vacant, pockmarked by windows sheathed with tin; other structures are still occupied but dreary, sad, and covered with graffiti. The landscape is bleak, the waste overwhelming.

Large parts of Brooklyn and Manhattan are just as bad. The landlords have left, and the tenants soon follow. New York City now holds more than 25,000 buildings whose owners long ago stopped paying taxes.

Visitors to the burned-out shell of a city-owned building in East Harlem walk gingerly, one at a time, up the rickety wooden stairs leading from the entryway to the third floor, where Lupe Torres lives with her two grandchildren.

Mrs. Torres, who has been here for two years, has tacked up oil-cloth and cardboard over the windows to help keep out the cold. Other tenants have nailed a large piece of plywood across a section of the hallway leading to a burned-out apartment. Despite the makeshift covering, a cold wind blows into the hall.

23

Mrs. Torres pays $115 a month for three rooms in this sixteen-apartment building the city took over two years ago.

"They want to send me to other apartments, but they're worse than this," she says.

In the midst of such devastation, small groups of tenants and community groups are succeeding where the private market long ago gave up and where government's traditional approaches have been pitifully inadequate.

Sixty-four West 175th Street in the South Bronx was abandoned by its owner one cold winter. Twenty-four families moved out, but twelve decided to stay. It took weeks to get the services restored because pipes had broken and ice had built up inside as well as outside the building. The tenants formed a council, pooled their rents, and, with help from the city's Emergency Repair Program, were able to restore services. Now twenty-two families live in the building, rents have increased, and the building is beginning to become self-sufficient again. In fact, the former owner wants it back.

Out of desperation and a determination not to be forced to flee again, small self-help groups organized by the tenants, neighborhood leaders, churches, and other voluntary agencies are achieving small-scale successes. They are becoming the landlords of last resort.[1]

Abandonment of older apartment buildings in New York City is a striking example of a process of disinvestment and decay that is national in scope. It affects whole neighborhoods as well as individual buildings; it affects single-family homes as well as apartments.

Abandonment provides a window on the interaction of various kinds of mediating structures and larger institutions. It is a tough testing ground for the concept that churches, voluntary associations, and neighborhood groups can make a difference and that policies should be changed so that "people-oriented" solutions can emerge.

Although New York City is the best-known case of large-scale abandonment, the same forces have been at work in city after city. In Newark whole neighborhoods are virtually gone; in Hartford the empty buildings of Clay Hill sit bricked up, mothballed like old warships; in Boston and Buffalo and in Chicago, the "city that works," once excellent apartments are now fuel for the arsonist rather than housing for families or an investment for a landlord. Even newer cities like Miami and Los Angeles suffer the same problems.

In each of these neighborhoods, in the midst of this devastation, small groups of tenants and individual owners are desperately trying to save their buildings and neighborhoods.

- In West Harlem, a coalition of a dozen block clubs and tenant groups is managing 500 units in twenty buildings. They have received $1 million from the city to rehabilitate fourteen additional buildings. They are now training and organizing tenants to identify and respond to landlord walkaways.
- In the Williamsburg section of Brooklyn, Los Sures, which began by leading tenant strikes, now manages 1,200 apartments in thirty-one buildings.
- The Northwest Bronx Community and Clergy Coalition has obtained agreements from neighborhood banks to halt foreclosures. In less than a year, they have fully repaired and rented five buildings with 150 apartments.
- On Manhattan's Lower East Side, Interfaith Adopt-A-Building has used "sweat equity" to renovate and manage more than thirty buildings. More than 300 persons have learned construction skills while rebuilding apartments.

In Chicago's Kenwood–Oakland area, St. Louis' North Side, and Philadelphia's Germantown, small self-help efforts are under way. Buildings are being saved that would otherwise be lost. Tenants are pooling their rents, learning how to budget for repairs, helping with maintenance and other management duties, and beginning to get other tenants to move back into vacant apartments so that the rent rolls will increase and security improve. These small signs of vitality are thus far mere flecks of light on a dark sea of abandonment. Like efforts by traditional owners to stay with their buildings in panic and hard times, these initiatives are doomed to fail unless they are given the economic and political support to enable them to increase the scale and success of their efforts.

THE CAUSES OF ABANDONMENT

There have been warning signs of abandonment and devastation for more than a decade, and the causes have been identified as threats to housing and neighborhoods for many years. Only very recently, however, have the full implications of this trend been recognized.

Furthermore, there is still little understanding of how various housing problems reinforce one another and finally cause abandonment. Until recent years each of these problems was seen in isolation—housing discrimination, redlining, the "milking" of buildings to earn short-term profits, the effects of rapid racial and class change in communities, and the resulting replacement of traditional institutions by newer, less effective ones. Few people have understood that these problems work together to destroy the tradition of private owners' interest in apartment buildings, causing landlords gradually to reduce services until tenants are left with a choice between moving and digging in to take on the ownership management and responsibilities themselves.

The widespread abandonment of housing began to attract public attention in the early 1970s. It had been recognized as a problem earlier in several cities, but the national implications had not been seen. The situation in New York City had attracted the most scrutiny, largely because the crisis in New York housing—like other crises in that city—was larger and more dramatic than the problems of smaller, less dense, and newer cities. Although some attributed the New York abandonment problem to rent control, which lessened the landlords' profits, it became clear that abandonment also occurred in many other cities that did not have rent control.

One national survey pointed to a series of broad urban economic, social, and racial changes as the causes of abandonment. Although there is still disagreement about details of this analysis, its overall outlines are now broadly accepted by analysts of urban change, public officials, and community groups involved in trying to stem decline.

The National Survey of Housing Abandonment described the process as follows:

> Housing obsolescence, the magnet of suburban residential and industrial development, increased tax rates and declining municipal services, erratic code enforcement and urban renewal programs set the stage for the racial and socioeconomic changes that have occurred in many American cities during the period since the mid-1940's. Racial change and the limited housing opportunities available to low-income minority people have provided, and continue to provide, real estate interests with short-term opportunities for over-crowding, decreased maintenance and increasing rents and sales prices. The profit-making is intense, but short-lived.
>
> At the same time that the market is exploited, perceived or threatened racial change accelerates disinvestment, first by the mortgage money market,

and second by owners. Real estate can no longer be sold or refinanced at competitive rates. Deterioration spirals as maintenance declines. Neighborhood flight accelerates, first by investors and then by the socially mobile, until only the poor, the aged, and the severely deprived remain.[2]

Disinvestment, or the withdrawal of capital investment in mortgages and improvement loans, is the final cause of decay. An owner finds he can no longer refinance his property on reasonable terms and earn a competitive return. Since income levels in the neighborhood are probably low and going lower, rent increases are difficult. The owner must therefore reduce his expectations of profit or reduce the level of services.

THE VULNERABILITY OF OLDER APARTMENT BUILDINGS

Although disinvestment and abandonment afflict neighborhoods of single-family homes, several factors make the situation of the apartment building owner different from that of a private homeowner. A private owner looks at his property not only for its investment value but also for its value as a home. Even if its investment value stabilizes or declines, he often does not want to move from the house or the neighborhood. On the other hand, the owner of investment property, such as an apartment building, typically does not live in the building and may not have strong personal ties to the building or its neighborhood. Any sign that its economic future may be uncertain or that alternative investments may be safer or more profitable may well lead to a decision to sell or abandon the property. Therefore, a neighborhood of multifamily buildings is especially susceptible to rapid changes in a time of economic decline.

Second, the viability of multifamily housing is strongly affected by the quality of its management. A decrease in the availability of competent management firms and maintenance and repair personnel —as is common in many cities—can have an unfavorable impact on living conditions and the long-range viability of the housing.

Third, the attitudes of tenants of any income level toward rental housing obviously differ from the attitudes of homeowners. It is unrealistic to expect tenants to invest the kind of time and resources in helping maintain their apartments that the average homeowner invests in his property. Furthermore, it is quite possible that the owner must contend with one or more "problem tenants" who willfully vandalize the building and aggravate its difficulties. These factors heighten the importance of the motivation and performance of the owner and manager in ensuring that the properties are well maintained.

Fourth, financial institutions often have inadequate knowledge of the economics and management of apartment buildings. These institutions are far better prepared to make investment decisions on single-family homes, where they need only judge the credit and character of the owner and the long-range value of the property. Asked to refinance apartment buildings, especially those whose future profitability is in doubt, they often are unprepared to analyze the long-range rent potential, expense, and cash flow of the buildings or the skill and capacity of the owner or manager. Many banks are inadequately informed about the economics of apartment buildings. As these financial institutions become nervous about neighborhood trends, or exercise inherent conservatism or institutional racism, they are apt to withdraw their mortgage and improvement funds more rapidly than they would from the more familiar family housing stock.

Fifth, the owners of apartment buildings tend to refinance frequently, entering into a new mortgage with amortization payments based on a twenty- or twenty-five-year payment period but with a large balloon payment due after eight or ten years. These loans are frequently not issued by financial institutions. This pattern of short-term financing means that disinvestment hits these buildings and neighborhoods more rapidly than it does single-family communities. Thus, when financial institutions and other lenders decide that a multifamily neighborhood is not attractive for investment, virtually all the buildings are directly affected in a relatively short time.

Meeting large balloon payments and still maintaining a large equity investment radically changes the profit picture for the owner. So does a speedup in the rate of amortization (by shortening the term from, say, ten to five years) or a shift to a higher-interest loan. The owner must increase his own investment (reducing his rate of return), or he must raise rents, reduce costs, or sell the building.

The most profitable approach, of course, is to reduce maintenance, cut back on repairs and improvements, and scrimp wherever possible. The final step in this almost inevitable "milking," or owner abandonment, process occurs when the owner decides to stop paying taxes. At that point the building is heading toward almost inevitable foreclosure and the great likelihood of demolition.

The traditional economics seldom work once it becomes impossible to refinance the property on reasonable terms and to obtain loans for improvements. The various megastructures—lenders, owners, and managers—have understandably withdrawn. The owner finds the most rational economic behavior is to take what he can and walk away. The likely results: one more vacant building, a dozen families displaced, another source of blight and panic in a neighborhood, and the loss of housing and capital investment that the nation desperately needs to conserve.

OWNERSHIP IN THE MOST DISTRESSED NEIGHBORHOODS

Even in the poorest, most abandoned multifamily communities there are usually at least a few buildings in which basic services are maintained and living conditions are decent. These buildings fall into five categories of ownership:

1. Public and federally assisted housing that is not subject to the same financial pressures as conventional buildings;
2. Buildings that are still well maintained by absentee owners whose commitments or financial positions are unique;
3. Small owner-occupied buildings;
4. Public ownership, which is growing in New York and many other cities that are witnessing a great increase in foreclosures on tax-delinquent apartment buildings (one section of New York's Lower East Side will soon be almost 70 percent publicly owned); and
5. Tenant and community ownership, which is also growing in several cities.

What are the prospects for each of these forms of ownership?

First, the nation's growing fiscal conservatism and skepticism about government programs, the enormous cost of federal housing programs, and the vastness of the abandonment problem make massive federal subsidies highly unlikely in the short range. At least in the immediate future only a relatively small proportion of inner city buildings is likely to be refinanced and subsidized with federal assistance.

Second, without a major change in federal policy, the economics of buildings in truly low-income neighborhoods will not support traditional absentee private ownership except in unique circumstances. The profits, if any, are too small and the alternative investments too attractive to allow such housing to attract investor-owners. (In contrast, in moderate-income areas in earlier stages of decline, the conventional private sector may still be willing and able to be the primary form of ownership.)

Third, local governments have little experience as landlords and little willingness or ability to assume this role over the long term. They face the difficulties arising from not having an owner or manager on the premises, able to observe and take action quickly on security, repair, maintenance, and tenant problems. They are severely hampered by slow and costly procurement and civil service restrictions. And they face relatively high expectations from tenants, who expect the city to bring buildings up to code and services up to standards, expectations that may not be possible considering their current conditions and city resources.

The most promising forms of ownership in these dire situations are owner-occupancy and community/tenant ownership. Yet without considerable resources, we do not have sufficient evidence of the viability of this course in large housing complexes over a long period of time.

OWNER-OCCUPIED BUILDINGS

Many studies have noted the commonsense fact that owner-occupied buildings tend to be better maintained than buildings owned by absentees. The accessibility of the owner to tenants with complaints, the owner's opportunity to observe maintenance or tenant problems firsthand, the owner's greater concern about the quality of services because of their effect on his own family, and the opportunity to develop good relations between the owner and the tenant all give owner-occupied buildings an advantage.

In Newark the Tri-City Citizens Union for Progress, which manages several hundred cooperative and rental units, pointed to the success of individual owners of FHA-financed three-flat houses in keeping up their buildings and providing good housing. The group stressed the importance of having a resident owner in the building as a way of ensuring that security and maintenance standards were maintained.

Los Sures in the Williamsburg section of Brooklyn has begun a very small program to develop resident ownership. After the group completed rehabilitation of a three-flat house with Comprehensive Employment and Training Act (CETA) laborers, one of the residents bought the house, entering into a contractual commitment to live in it, maintain it well, and keep the rents reasonable. The organization hopes to duplicate this approach on several other houses, building a cadre of resident-owners who will add stability to the neighborhood. Hartford's Upper Albany Community Organization is following a similar approach.

Yet resident owners have problems. In West Harlem, for example, the executive director of the West Harlem Community Organization recounted the difficulties of a person living in one of six townhouses he owned on 116th Street. The owner "poured every cent he could back into the buildings," devoting a great deal of his own time to repairs and maintenance. However, like other small owners in New York, this man found himself ineligible for rehabilitation assistance under any city program and was without a source of expert technical assistance as he sought loan funds and tax concessions and tackled management problems.[3]

In responding to abandonment, government agencies have paid little attention to the need to support owner-occupants of buildings in marginal neighborhoods. At a meeting of two task forces of the National Commission on Neighborhoods, an organization representing such small owners complained bitterly about this neglect. It urged that loan, rehabilitation, management assistance programs, and city eviction policies be modified so that such owners would have a better chance to maintain their buildings as decent housing.

COMMUNITY MANAGEMENT AND OWNERSHIP

Tenants in many buildings quickly decide that the best thing to do is escape the decay by moving to another apartment farther from the vortex of the storm. Increasingly, however, tenants who have already moved two or three or five times have decided they cannot escape so easily. They have decided to stay and fight to make their buildings livable.

These people actually have little choice. No one else is prepared to manage the buildings or to take on ownership responsibilities; so a community group must either watch the building be vacated and torn down or must respond to the demands of its own constituency and take over management responsibility.

There are a great many forms of what can generally be referred to as "community management." These range from extralegal or legally recognized rent strikes, in which rents are placed in escrow and used to restore services, to tenant management, to court appointment of community administrators for neglected properties, to community receivers, to community groups that acquire the property from the owner or local government by purchase or donation. To add to the complexity, a single building may go through all these and other stages, often existing in an extralegal never-never land where the owner has "disowned" the building and the community group or tenants have provided services without having a legal right to play any role in management.

Most frequently, the groups that take on these responsibilities emerge from a history of tenant organizing and tenant strikes. When the boiler finally breaks down, or the pipes burst, or a paid arsonist appears, the tenants react in desperation and either organize themselves or, more frequently, seek help from a local community group. The organization then begins to become inextricably involved in management. First, it begins to pool the rents, keeping them in reserve as a bargaining chip for negotiating with the landlord. Second, if the owner has finally decided to walk away from the building completely, bargaining becomes impossible, and a new management arrangement becomes necessary. Finding conventional managers as uninterested in the properties as traditional owners, the group then has little choice but to take on management responsibilities itself. The owner becomes increasingly irrelevant; since he has no interest in the building, he does not object to this change; and the community managers deal directly with the tenants and others, bypassing the landlord. The situation differs from squatting in that no one objects to the new arrangement, and a de facto collective management emerges.

Los Sures and West Harlem

Los Sures's experience in Williamsburg, Brooklyn, is quite typical of the more highly organized and successful community management groups. A Hispanic community organization, Los Sures was originally a community management project. It quickly turned into a nonprofit organization with a much broader community purpose.

Los Sures started with traditional organizing tactics, including rent strikes, but it found that rent strikes drive landlords away rather than bring them to the bargaining table. The organization concluded that it must take on management and maintenance responsibilities. In 1978 it was managing thirty-one buildings, with approximately 1,200 units. It receives funds from the city's Community Management Program, federal manpower training programs, and other sources.

In West Harlem, each winter brings on a surge of organizing among tenants who find themselves without heat. Rather than move, they turn increasingly to tenant organizations and tenant management as at least a temporary solution to the management vacuum. They call rent strikes, pooling their normal rents in a common fund to pay for maintenance. They turn to the city for emergency repair of their heating systems, turn to the courts for the appointment of a tenant manager, and turn to themselves to make the building livable again. As a result, the West Harlem Community Organization, which began as a volunteer organization, is taking on formal management responsibilities for large numbers of buildings. It is obtaining city, state, and federal funds to employ neighborhood residents to organize tenants, to renovate apartments, and to provide daily maintenance. Its goal is the eventual transfer of ownership and management responsibilities either to the community organization or to tenant cooperatives.

Morris Heights

The same sort of action is taking place in many other communities in New York and other cities. In the Morris Heights section of the Bronx, the Neighborhood Improvement Association sought and obtained a city contract to take over management responsibility for thirty-three apartment buildings deserted by their owners but not yet taken over by the city through tax foreclosure. In each of those buildings, one or two tenants had come to the Neighborhood Improvement Association asking for help in dealing with serious management problems. The association had sent the tenants back to their buildings to find out whether their problems were shared by others and whether the tenants as a group were willing to take on management duties. Once the findings were made, the organization sent an organizer into the building to meet with the tenants, to ascertain their immediate needs, and to discuss strategies for restoring services and attracting tenants into vacant apartments.

Like community groups involved in similar work, the Morris Heights Neighborhood Association focuses heavily on tenant education. After the initial organizing meetings, the association holds a series of training sessions for the tenants. These begin with a thorough discussion of rents, repair and maintenance, and the need for the tenants to work with the association in preparing a building budget. There is heavy emphasis on having all tenants pay their rents promptly and especially on requiring payment from tenants who had refused to pay rent when the building had no services. Later sessions focus on the attraction and selection of new tenants, the need to evict tenants who do not pay their rents or whose behavior is unacceptable to their neighbors, ways of cutting unnecessary expenses, involvement of tenants in reducing security problems, and other nuts-and-bolts issues. The training includes thorough and continuing discussion of the long-range future and especially of the ownership and management arrangements most desirable from the tenants' point of view.

The positive results—and the limitations—of these efforts are clear. After one year of experience with formal management responsibilities, the Morris Heights Neighborhood Improvement Association described two buildings as follows:

47 West 175th Street. This 26 unit building, located on the same block, remains the only other occupied multiple dwelling on the block of landlord abandoned buildings. The tenancy in this building was down to seven and a vacate order had been placed on the building. Other neighborhood residents assisted the tenants to clear up violations and through the help of the Litigation Bureau the vacate order was removed. Owned by the same owner as 64 West 175th Street, this building's tenants committed themselves to saving their home. They now have a total of 16 families and a viable building. They have increased their cash flow from $900 per month to $1800. An Administrator is also serving and the building has been tentatively approved for 309 Receivership.

The efforts of the tenants in the building have not only saved their building but have prevented home owners from fleeing the block.

1600 Nelson Avenue. This 26-unit building came to us requesting assistance approximately three years ago after experiencing serious problems with repairs and services before their owner walked away—A tenant in the building became administrator. The building was well organized and worked very closely with this organization. Over a year ago the building went into City Ownership and is now being managed by DRE. Application has been made for Community Management and the building has been accepted into the program. The building has experienced serious problems of inadequate services under DRE management and the tenants are anxiously awaiting transfer into Community Management.[4]

A score of other groups are taking on similar responsibilities elsewhere. These include church groups, such as the congregations of St. John's Church and the Memorial Baptist Church in Harlem, whch have worked with tenants to save buildings next to their properties.

All these efforts are limited, but they are producing results. They are reducing turnover, reoccupying largely vacated buildings, and motivating tenants to take on big jobs rather than flee and thus "disinvest" their neighborhoods of human resources.

AN ENORMOUS BURDEN

The tenant organizations, community groups, and churches that have taken on these responsibilities have assumed enormous burdens. They have taken on extraordinarily difficult management duties: the buildings have been milked, their services cut off; the tenants often consider themselves transient and without a stake in the building or neighborhood; the private and public sectors have turned their backs on the community; and crime and other social problems are legion.

The resource picture is equally bleak. New York City offers aid to self-help management groups, but few other city governments provide any financial, management, or other expert assistance to groups trying to keep buildings afloat. The legal work alone is enough to frighten community groups, especially those that depend heavily on volunteers with few managerial skills. The ownership of these buildings is in a legal no man's land: the owner has left the building but still theoretically has ownership responsibilities, and city government and the courts go through a slow process of foreclosure and eventual takeover of ownership. This process can take from two to eight years, depending on local procedures. The community groups also have to wrestle with a series of complicated legal questions related to the rights of tenants who are not receiving services in return for their rents, the rights of tenants to place their rents in escrow and to pay for their own services, and the rights of tenants to remain in a foreclosed building. Then there are receivership procedures and remedies, and finally—if the tenants do succeed in charting a way toward eventual self-ownership and self-management —the difficulties remain of meeting the legal requirements for non-profit, cooperative, or condominium ownership.

Added to these difficulties are the problems of running a building on limited income. Code standards, some tenants' unrealistically high expectations of building services, the complexities of obtaining financing for rehabilitation and carrying out that rehabilitation without displacing tenants, the difficulties of getting reliable repair companies to provide services in neighborhoods considered unsafe— all of these problems plague groups trying to take on self-help management responsibilities.

The resources are seldom there. The rents are not sufficient to support a community organization's initial work in maintaining buildings until they are minimally self-sufficient, in assisting with legal, technical, and rehabilitation questions, and in working on other vital neighborhood issues. Technical assistance is hard to find. Even in New York City, which has the most sophisticated set of programs to help community groups, there is only minimum assistance on management problems, legal questions, and rehabilitation. There is instead a series of fragmented programs, each mired in red tape.

LACK OF SUPPORT

The West Harlem Community Organization (WHCO) provides an example of what could politely be termed a lack of systematic support. Although WHCO has successfuly managed almost a dozen buildings and is in the process of rehabilitating several of them and although it is generally considered an exceptionally responsible organization that deserves city program support, the organization sits in the middle of a quagmire of bureaucracy. The executive director, Margaret McNeill, a black woman in her fifties, has devoted fifteen years of her life to running the organization and to helping tenants keep their buildings as nearly viable as possible.

From 1968 to early 1978, Mrs. McNeill sought adequate resources to support a major community management program. Each winter WHCO would become the de facto manager of buildings without heat and other services. The organization struggled along, with Mrs. McNeill receiving a full salary some years, far less in other years. WHCO had no funds for other professional staff. Finally, in 1978, WHCO received a city contract that allowed it to employ thirty-eight people from the community to take on organizing, management, and rehabilitation of some of the buildings. WHCO also received a sizeable city grant that allowed it to hire additional administrative and bookkeeping help, as well as maintenance personnel. However, the city did not give it sufficient funds to hire middle-level staff to help supervise the new trainees and to oversee the management and rehabilitation efforts the organization is undertaking. They had to turn to churches for this crucial money.

The red tape is classic. WHCO is required to have nine separate bank accounts. Trainees can be used on some buildings but not on others, including those buildings WHCO manages under city contract. Only individuals, rather than organizations, can be appointed by the courts to be administrators of buildings after the owners have cut off services; but only organizations can take on the responsibility of managing buildings that then fall into foreclosure and city ownership. Despite the city's reliance on community groups to manage some of its 25,000 buildings, its policies favor sale of acquired buildings at the highest possible price, often to speculators who will immediately remove the community organizations and tenants from management but then will fail to deliver adequate services. A property disposition program, geared to negotiated sales to the tenants themselves, has been in existence for three years but has never closed a sale.

Such horror stories involving WHCO could go on and on. There is the fine old courtyard building, still fully occupied and in relatively good condition, that the city will not allow WHCO to rehabilitate unless it replaces the old-fashioned elevator (at a cost of $37,000). Renovation, maintenance, and continued occupancy would otherwise be possible, but this code requirement makes rehabilitation impracticable and is likely to lead to the demolition of the building. And there are the welfare tenants who are not allowed to place their rents in escrow despite the fact that this would ensure that their building would be well maintained.

A NEW DIRECTION

Mediating structures have succeeded in cases where government and private megastructures have failed. They have not proved they are the answer to the total problem, but they have shown that they can reduce turnover, lead to the management of "unmanageable" buildings, create a level of social control, and reduce expectations concerning the quality of services, and otherwise stabilize conditions. The key policy question is whether society will find ways to support these fledgling tenant and community efforts to save one building at a time, so that eventually these efforts may lead to saving thousands of buildings.

A system of relatively limited amounts of financial aid, together with highly skilled help with legal, managerial, and other technical problems, would give these groups a chance to succeed on a larger scale. This last point is of great importance, for the community institutions that have emerged to take on these problems are the very institutions that show promise of being able to tackle some of the other pressing problems of social disorganization and decay in low-income urban neighborhoods. These organizations have begun to reduce crime among juveniles, to increase discipline and motivation in the schools, to press for more adequate public services in the neighborhoods, and to demand that financial institutions invest in the neighborhoods and in housing whenever feasible. Since the decay of neighborhoods has led to the elimination of the traditional economic, political, and social institutions that hold the social fabric together, it is essential that the community organizations that are beginning to re-create this undergirding be given support as they try to fill the vacuum left by traditional apartment owners and managers.

As these mediating structures seek to cope with the disastrous consequences of past policy and of inaction, they show how small, grass-roots efforts with a real community base can begin to overcome many of the destructive activities of the megastructures. At the very least, they represent an innovative approach that shows far more promise than the failures of the past. With adequate support, they could become forerunners of a new policy of self-determination, self-help, and community renewal.

REFERENCES

1. Andrew Mott (co-author), recollection of site visit to South Bronx, 1978.
2. Center for Community Change and National Urban League, *National Survey of Housing Abandonment* (Washington, D.C.: 1971), p. 1.
3. National Commission on Neighborhoods, Neighborhood Revitalization Report (unpublished staff report, Washington, D.C., 1979), p. 29.
4. Morris Heights Association, Analysis of Morris Heights (unpublished report to City Planning Department, New York, 1977).

4 AVOIDING ANOTHER MARQUETTE PARK

Folks at the border of Marquette Park saw the change coming [for] [sic] more than two years ago.

A big red "For Sale" sign hung over the Moose Lodge on Western Avenue. Someone kept stealing the wire trash basket in front of the dime store and litter cluttered the street.

Flower shop owner Steve Gay found a gaping rut in the parkway outside his shop's door, but the city failed to repair it.

A grocery store, a bakery, a stationery shop, an insurance company and a dress shop along Western Avenue closed their doors, few of them to be replaced.

The streets fell into disrepair. When the first few blacks moved in, weeds grew longer and the garbage man stopped coming around twice a week. Residents white and black grew nervous.

"The neighborhood's gonna go down," Mrs. Schanell Willis, a black who moved in last May, said angrily. "They don't even clean the streets. They dug holes in the street for the gas line. Do you think they came back and cleaned them up?"

James Stampley, who bought a home in the neighborhood for his daughter, said he had to complain repeatedly to get the city to cut the weeds by the railroad tracks near her home. When she first moved in, he said, the weeds were cut regularly.

Black residents complained that the police officers were biased, and following violence in the area, UPI learned that a human relations officer recommended to the city that the police force be replaced with officers

41

from outside the district. More than 75 per cent of the officers currently live in the district. The recommendation was ignored.

Across the tracks in the black neighborhood of West Englewood, residents were having a worse time. Their streets were swept but the sewers were clogged, trees were untrimmed and street curbing eroded until it cracked.

This autumn, a citizen's group determined to fight back, noting the spiffy appearance of trim curbing in the white area across Western.

On September 30, members of the Concerned Citizens of Southwest Englewood paraded to the office of Democratic Ward Committeeman Frank Savickas. On his steps, they left a dead rat, a 100 pound chunk of eroded curbing, a tree branch and an old couch.

Savickas, a state senator who lives in all-white Marquette Park, is the chief neighborhood decision maker on such city services.

"Frank Savickas refuses to meet over in our area," said Willie Starks, a spokesperson for the community group. "He meets with white people, but not with black people."

But the day after the protest, the community group rejoiced. City workers suddenly began digging holes in the streets of West Englewood to rod out the sewers.

It was a month before the election.[1]

For Sale signs dominate many neighborhoods across the country as America continues to wrestle with racial and economic change. All too often neighborhoods change diametrically, from all white to all black or from all poor to all upper income, as people's fears and economic forces combine to make it extraordinarily difficult to achieve racial and economic integration. In the Washington, D.C., area, for example, as large parts of suburban Prince George's County rapidly turn black, racial trends in the District of Columbia are reversing, even such historically black neighborhoods as L'Edroit Park undergoing speculative renovation that results in displacement of lower-income blacks.

The otherwise obscure Chicago neighborhood of Marquette Park focused attention for several months in 1977 on one part of this tragedy of resegregation. Firebombings, marches, and counter-marches shook Marquette Park that year. Civil rights groups and black organizations demonstrated for housing opportunities for blacks; other organizations, including the Ku Klux Klan and the American Nazi Party, staged protests against the rapid racial change occurring in the community.

Although Marquette Park is an extreme example of the tension and resegregation that can result from neighborhood transition, what happened there has occurred in countless neighborhoods.

America has become familiar with the scenario in which the individual prejudices of the members of a community have been reinforced by forces that profit by aggravating racial and economic fears and stimulating the rapid turnover that results in resegregation.

Neighborhoods going through such transition provide significant case studies for contrasting the roles of megastructures and mediating structures vis-à-vis neighborhood conservation and housing policy. In community after community, powerful private and public institutions have, through acts of commission and omission, exerted a devastating influence on worthwhile housing and on the whole of neighborhood life. In many of these communities, church groups, block clubs, neighborhood associations, and other voluntary organizations have been the only vehicles through which residents have been able to assert their own interests and values. Although such groups vary widely in their responses to change and in their scope, effectiveness, and resources, they share a common role in mediating between the interests of local families and the interests of more powerful private and public institutions that lack accountability to, or concern about, a particular neighborhood.

MARQUETTE PARK'S CRISIS

Marquette Park was for years a classic "ethnic" neighborhood. Populated by Lithuanians, Italians, and other white working-class families, the community had been a stable area with strong cultural, religious, and educational institutions. Over the decades, Marquette Park had been an exceptionally close community, united by churches, fraternal associations, cultural and language ties, and ethnic stores and restaurants.

The neighborhood was redlined a few years ago. Fearing that blacks from neighboring Englewood would soon begin buying homes in Marquette Park, most financial institutions reduced their lending in the area. Several banks and savings and loan associations translated their natural fiscal conservatism into discrimination as they altered their policies. The results? Discrimination and a grave threat to the value and viability of the neighborhood's housing stock.

Insurance companies also discriminated against the area. According to one banker, these companies raised Chicago inner city homeowner's insurance rates to an annual average of $616 for a thirty-five-year-old brick house while charging owners of similar suburban homes only $108. Inner city automobile insurance also jumped, further increasing the financial burden on residents of older neighborhoods.

Homeowners suffering these new burdens then met the block-busters. Dozens of new real estate offices opened in Marquette Park. Billboards, leaflets, and telephone calls bombarded residents, advocating selling before prices fell lower. As sales rose, so did the number of real estate commissions. In 1975 and 1976, the rate of turnover became extraordinary. In one thirty-six-block area in Marquette Park, the number of homes sold increased ninefold, from 11 in 1974 to 106 in 1976.

In the same period the insuring activity of the Federal Housing Administration (FHA) increased by 800 percent. Real estate agents directed potential buyers to FHA-insured loans, which offered low down payment, 100 percent guaranteed mortgages. As FHA-insured loans supplanted conventional financing, private financial institutions further reduced their stake and their confidence in Marquette Park. The percentage of homes insured by FHA went from 64 percent (seven of eleven homes) to 100 percent (ninety-six of ninety-six homes) between 1974 and 1976.

The vast majority of the FHA-insured homes were purchased by blacks. Within less than two years, half of the white families in an 1,100-home area had fled, and many of the remaining white-owned homes were for sale.

A six-month investigation by two United Press International (UPI) reporters concluded:

> Racial steering was widespread in the Marquette Park area. This is how it worked:
>
> • Until the first blacks moved in, real estate agents sold homes in the area only to whites or Spanish-speaking people. They waited until black brokers sold to the first blacks.
> • Once the change began, dozens of real estate agents set up offices near the area and concentrated on peddling homes to blacks. They avoided showing homes in the changing area to whites. They offered no listings in nearby white areas to black buyers.
> • Most brokers in the adjacent all-white neighborhood sold no homes to blacks, limiting the selection for blacks to the changing area.
> • The real estate agents used the Federal Housing Administration and Veterans Administration mortgage insurance programs almost exclu--sively. They encouraged blacks to use FHA and VA insurance, and encouraged white sellers to use government insurance programs, even though it cost more.[2]

The UPI reporters investigated the sale and resale of twenty-five homes in nearby West Englewood. They found that speculators bought them at an average of $7,900 and sold them at an average of $18,000 under the government insurance programs. One of the most dramatic cases involved a house purchased for $3,000 and resold for $19,000 without substantial improvement.

Despite the startling increase in the use of FHA insurance in the neighborhood, the raging blockbusting and speculation, and the danger that racial panic would lead to a resegregated (black rather than integrated) neighborhood, the FHA took no action to alleviate the situation. In fact, subsequent interviews with federal officials and others revealed that FHA officials were far less informed than community groups, newspaper reporters, and civil rights organizations about the impact of their insuring programs.

HUD acted only after violence erupted. Firebombings and intimidation had accompanied racial change in Marquette Park. The leader of the Nazis proclaimed: "I would rather have a race war where people are killing each other and lobbing hand grenades at each other, than have a system where everybody lived peacefully together and brought up their children to race mix with one another."[3] On July 17, 1976, in the midst of civil rights marches and antiblack countermarches, fifteen policemen and thirteen others were injured. Sixty-three persons were arrested. The violence continued for months.

With the exception of the FHA, which eventually may lose millions of dollars because of risky loans in the area, each of the institutions that played an active role in the transformation of Marquette Park acted in its own interest. Real estate agents, bankers, and mortgage bankers reaped large profits. The FHA saw itself as strengthening the housing market and housing opportunity by responding to a demand for mortgage insurance, especially among black and other minority families, but none of these institutions was structured to be accountable to neighborhood people or to be concerned about the future of the neighborhood or its housing stock. Each was an outsider, largely unconcerned about the social and economic effect of its actions on the neighborhood.

This is not to say that there were not real estate agents or financial institutions or public officials who were concerned about what was happening. Some individuals in each of these fields rose above their own apparent short-term self-interest, either on their own initiative or under neighborhood pressure, and made decisions helpful to the neighborhood and its housing. Some neighborhood real estate brokers, for example, refused to "panic peddle," advertised widely, and stressed the availability of conventional as well as FHA-insured financing in the neighborhood. Some financial institutions not only kept making loans in the neighborhood, but joined together in neighborhood-based initiatives to stimulate reinvestment and rehabilitation. And some FHA officials were distressed by the agency's performance as it proceeded to sanction activity in Marquette Park without regard to fair housing or neighborhood welfare.

These individuals were not enough to offset the pressure the megastructures placed on the community. Institutions created such rapid, artificially stimulated, racially oriented change that the eventual result was bound to be resegregation, the eventual flight of middle-income blacks, and, later, a wave of defaults leading to abandonment.

Marquette Park illustrates how American housing policy often fosters segregation, racial strife, fraud, and tremendous losses to the federal treasury. As a classic case of the role private and public megastructures can play in undermining responsible housing policy, it provides a good background for analyzing why these forces operate as they do and how their behavior might be changed. It also provides a setting for looking at the roles mediating structures can play in helping transitional neighborhoods reconcile the goal of housing opportunities for minorities with the goal of conserving the quality of local housing and neighborhood institutions. The roles of mediating structures are examined later in this chapter.

REAL ESTATE BROKERS

Underlying the situation in Marquette Park and the overall problem of housing opportunities for minorities is the force of the "dual housing market." In most cities housing opportunities are effectively separated into two markets—one for whites, the other for minorities. The dual market is based on two separate systems of supply and demand that reinforce, and indeed thrive on, geographic segregation.

Each side of the dual system is characterized by different sets of actors in the fields of real estate brokerage and finance. Blacks generally go to black brokers or to "transition specialists" who provide them with listings for black or transitional neighborhoods;

whites go through an equally segregated system. Information on available housing is often gathered and listed by section of the city, reflecting segregated living patterns, and brokers subscribe only to those listing services that provide information on the side of the dual market they have chosen to serve.

In Marquette Park, for example, the UPI investigation of real estate firms found that eleven of fourteen realty firms employed selective referral techniques. White people testing referral patterns used by those eleven firms were given listings in the white areas and blacks were not, or blacks were shown homes in the area targeted for resegregation and whites were not.

Besides this racial "steering," the real estate agents directed prospective buyers to FHA- and VA-insured loans rather than conventional loans. According to the UPI survey, "Most sellers were under the impression that no conventional home loan money was available and at least thirteen said real estate agents advised that they use FHA and VA financing." A local banker stated:

> Now we are fairly certain that real estate brokers will infiltrate the area telling the people that they could only sell their homes with FHA insured mortgages. That being the case, anybody that would want to purchase, or even the people that were living there now that wanted to sell, would not make any attempt to seek out conventional financing. You see the obvious physical effects—board-up and the merchants start leaving.[4]

The former chief of the FHA's Chicago Area Single Family Mortgage Credit Division agreed: "Sure, the realtors are the ones that steer them into FHA."

THE FEDERAL HOUSING ADMINISTRATION AND VETERANS ADMINISTRATION PROGRAMS

The FHA and VA insurance programs have provided an invaluable opportunity for millions of families to buy homes with low down payments and twenty-five, thirty, or forty years to complete their mortgage payments. They have been largely responsible for the enormous suburban housing boom over the last four decades. They have also been an increasing source of housing opportunities for blacks and other minorities in the last few years, after eliminating such earlier discriminatory practices as racial covenants and appraisals based in part on a neighborhood's racial character.

These programs have also provided unscrupulous real estate brokers and unethical or careless lenders with excellent means for increasing their profits. The programs rely heavily on the lender to screen the risks. A low-income family is not barred from purchasing a home by its lack of savings because the required down payments are so small. The crucial question then becomes whether the family's income is sufficient to make mortgage payments and cover taxes, repairs, insurance, utilities, and other obligations. The primary responsibility for checking lies with the lender, which, being completely insured against loss if the homebuyer defaults, has little financial incentive to screen homebuyers' income and assets carefully. Against this background, unscrupulous brokers have a tempting opportunity to increase their sales volume. It is entirely predictable that, facing this temptation, some brokers step up blockbusting and help low-income people misrepresent their income and savings to obtain federally insured mortgages.

The results of this pattern of abusing government housing programs are defaults and foreclosures, empty homes open to vandalism and arson, and demoralization of neighborhoods.

MORTGAGE BANKERS

Mortgage bankers originate about 75 percent of all FHA-insured mortgages. In 1975 they authorized more than $80 billion in federally protected mortgage loans.

The mortgage banking industry is little known to the public. Mortgage bankers make long-term loans but—unlike banks, savings and loan associations, savings banks, or credit unions—do not handle deposits from customers. They function primarily as intermediaries between local real estate brokers and distant investors who put large amounts of money into housing loans and find it useful to use locally based agents who specialize in finding people who want to borrow money to buy, improve, or refinance a house. Mortgage bankers typically develop strong working relationships with particular real estate agents.

The introduction of the FHA and its mortgage insurance programs in 1934 launched the development of the modern mortgage banking industry. As one noted economist has remarked, "Mortgage companies . . . are essentially a result, though not a planned one, of the Federal government's underwriting of residential mortgages."[5]

Mortgage companies have become specialists in the FHA and VA markets—issuing and packaging mortgages, handling government paperwork, securing funds from insurance companies and others, and developing strong contacts with local real estate brokers. Philip E. Kidd, an economist for the Mortgage Bankers Association, has explained the industry's relationship to the FHA/VA programs: "Throughout long years of working with FHA and VA programs, mortgage bankers have developed valuable contacts and insights about the federal bureaucracy that helped turn their proposals into operating procedures."[6]

This obscure industry is largely unregulated. Only two states have enacted laws specifically regulating some aspects of its operations. Furthermore, mortgage bankers are not within the jurisdiction of the banking regulatory agencies unless they are subsidiaries of banks or bank holding companies.

The burden of regulating mortgage bankers falls solely on the Department of Housing and Urban Development (HUD). The department grants approval to firms to participate as lenders in HUD's mortgage insurance programs and occasionally withdraws approval from questionable firms. But there is a fundamental conflict between HUD's central commitment to encourage housing production and lower interest rates by maximizing loan volume and its commitment to regulate lenders to ensure high loan-underwriting standards. Can a government agency whose primary goal is to generate housing also regulate in the interests of the consumer? Probably not, no more than General Motors could logically set safety and environmental standards or the Teamsters Union set standards for accountability to its members. HUD's regulatory system is marked by a "clumsy, snail-like manner of proceeding, inadequate definitions regarding what constitutes conduct warranting the withdrawal of approval, confusion concerning what remedies should be dispensed, and failure to implement follow-up monitoring of the lenders' compliance."[7] In the words of the House Committee on Government Operations, "HUD's monitoring of mortgage servicing practices has been largely ineffective."[8]

It is the regulated mortgage banking megastructure that is responsible for issuing 75 percent of the FHA-insured loans, with sometimes devastating consequences for neighborhoods. Because FHA insurance provides a 100 percent guarantee against loss from foreclosure and because each FHA mortgage generates a substantial fee, there is a strong incentive for high-volume, rapid loan production. It is not surprising that less scrupulous firms have lent to people with inadequate income and credit or that they have co-operated with real estate brokers who have sold homes in such bad condition that it is predictable that the buyers will eventually walk away and stop payment. The insured lender is assured that the property will be taken off his hands by HUD quickly and at full value. The lender therefore has little incentive to work with a home-owner who is having difficulty making payments, to counsel that person on budgeting funds and catching up on house payments, or to seek agreement on recasting the mortgage to extend the pay-ments over a longer period of time to avoid foreclosure.

The incentives toward maximizing the quantity of sales and mortgage loans reinforce the dual housing market. Although preju-dice and acts of discrimination on the part of individual homeowners —such as refusal to sell a home to a black family or moving away because a neighborhood is becoming integrated—play a role, the behavior of the private and public megastructures has a much stronger effect on housing and neighborhood patterns.

THE FEDERAL RESPONSE TO MARQUETTE PARK

Disturbed and embarrassed by the violence and the national atten-tion given to Marquette Park, HUD finally took action in early 1977. The department required all applicants for FHA insurance for Marquette Park homes first go through a homebuyer's counseling program that briefed them on their right to buy homes anywhere in metropolitan Chicago and on the responsibilities and expenses of homeownership. Measures were taken to ensure that the houses they were considering were sound and worth the asking price. This counseling program put brokers and mortgage bankers on notice that HUD and homebuyers were being especially vigilant in Marquette Park and thus deterred them from some of the more egregious abuses.

At the same time, the department established a Marquette Park Task Force composed of several middle-level Washington staff members who were ordered to investigate the situation and make recommendations to Secretary Harris of HUD on changes in FHA policies that could help the department avoid future Marquette

Parks. Secretary Harris announced that she would make an important statement on future FHA neighborhood policy at the end of that ninety-day study. Upon hearing of the creation of this task force, Mrs. Gale Cincotta, the nationally known antiredlining leader, remarked: "It is sad and ironic that, after ignoring redlining and the abuse of FHA programs for years, HUD is finally jarred into action by the Nazis and the KKK."[9]

The task force assigned staff and a consultant team to analyze the Marquette Park situation and draft recommendations. After an initial period of great activity, the task force began to lose momentum. Sensing this change, members of the consulting group issued a direct challenge to the department in their final report: "Will the Department limit its response to situations like Marquette Park to firefighting? Or will it instead institute a series of rather fundamental changes which will advance housing opportunities and neighborhood vitality in transitional and declining neighborhoods generally?"[10]

HUD pulled back from development of new FHA policies as the clamor subsided in Marquette Park, because the counseling program was greatly reducing FHA loan activity in the neighborhood. To some it appeared as if HUD wanted to avoid any responsibility in the area, for either past or future problems.

The ninety-day deadline passed, and the secretary made no public statement on future FHA policy toward neighborhoods. Business continued as usual. HUD ducked the responsibility of dealing seriously with the ways in which the FHA and the VA could be restructured to eliminate abuses and to reconcile apparently competing equal opportunity and neighborhood conservation interests. No effort was made either to exert control over the megastructures that were adding to Marquette Park's problems or to strengthen the local community groups and other mediating structures that were trying to reconcile those interests.

THE LOCAL GOVERNMENT RESPONSE

The city of Chicago played little direct role in Marquette Park. It added police to cope with the violence but made no special efforts to allocate additional funds, services, or specialized staff to the community to help neighborhood and civil rights groups struggle with the complexities of one of America's most serious continuing problems—how to balance housing opportunity and neighborhood conservation goals. It thus left these mediating structures without significant government advice or assistance.

Even more important, the city has consistently avoided the central issues of the roles of major private sector institutions in aggravating and profiting from situations like Marquette Park's. Local officials have made no effort to crack down on unscrupulous and discriminatory practices by elements of the real estate and mortgage banking industries and by conventional lenders.

MEDIATING STRUCTURES IN
NEIGHBORHOODS LIKE MARQUETTE PARK

Various types of mediating structures respond in different ways to situations such as that in Marquette Park. One series of responses has been exclusionary. In many white communities, neighborhood groups have emerged to fight racial integration. In many white, integrated, and minority neighborhoods there has been equally vociferous opposition to economic integration. From opposition to public housing in Coney Island, to total opposition to FHA-insured loans in sections of Chicago, to great acrimony over the most elementary advances in "fair housing" in Warren, Michigan, some neighborhood organizations and voluntary associations have "mediated" on behalf of neighborhood stabilization policies that clearly sought to exclude minority and low-income people.

Another series of responses has been integrationist. Mediating structures have been in the forefront of integration efforts in every city. Since the civil rights marches in the South, the National Association for the Advancement of Colored People (NAACP), the Urban League, and many allied church, public interest, and neighborhood groups have been leading proponents of greater housing opportunities. They have fought for changes in real estate and lending practices through marches, political action, legislation, litigation, and pilot programs. They have pressed for an end to discrimination in its various forms, including steering, blockbusting, redlining, and the FHA's racial covenants. In taking the initiative on these issues, they often face vehement opposition from the private and public institutions that reinforce the dual housing market.

A third response by mediating structures has been to promote reforms of the megastructures, including reforms in FHA programs, real estate and mortgage banking policies, and local government priorities. The reforms promoted with some success by such groups as Chicago's Metropolitian Area Housing Alliance have included more careful FHA inspection and appraisal policies, tougher license requirements for real estate brokers, regulation of mortgage bankers, new public programs to stimulate reinvestment of private mortgage and home improvement funds in declining neighborhoods, and increased public investment and services in these areas.

The fourth response by mediating structures has been to create new services to help neighborhoods meet the challenge of opening housing opportunities while maintaining the equilibrium of the community and its housing. Such responses have ranged from block clubs to alternative vehicles for real estate brokerage, financing, rehabilitation, and maintenance.

PROMOTION OF FAIR HOUSING AND FAIR LENDING

In Marquette Park the groups promoting fair housing ranged from the Southern Christian Leadership Conference, to human relations agencies that came together to try to quell the violence of 1976, to the Leadership Council on Metropolitan Housing Opportunities, which has fought through the courts for more than a decade to obtain bans on racial steering and other discriminatory real estate practices, to the merchants' associations that tried to keep the commercial strips in Marquette Park viable.

One of the largest struggles has been over mortgage redlining. This confrontation has provided a particularly dramatic example of the potential of mediating structures.

Before 1970 concern with redlining and disinvestment was confined to relatively few people. Jane Jacobs' seminal book *The Death and Life of Great American Cities* pointed to "credit blacklisting" as a practice that drained the lifeblood from neighborhoods.[11] A 1961 report by the U.S. Commission on Civil Rights stated that lending institutions "are a major factor in denial of equal housing opportunity" and concluded bluntly that "banks dictate where Negroes can live."[12] The commission documented many examples of credit discrimination: Detroit banks were not willing to approve loans that would enable blacks to buy homes in white neighborhoods; San Francisco banks outlined areas where blacks would be denied loans; in Columbus, Ohio, where nonwhites did obtain mortgages, they were required to accept shorter terms and make higher down payments. (Nevertheless, the federal government's Kaiser Commission, Douglas Commission, and other public explorations of housing problems later in the 1960s generally bypassed the issue of discrimination in housing finance and focused instead on housing production needs.)

In the early 1970s local mediating structures, especially community organizations, block clubs, and churches, began to give increasing attention to the redlining problem. As early as 1971 a sustained grass-roots antiredlining campaign had begun in Chicago. A year later 2,000 persons representing neighborhood groups and churches in thirty-six states and seventy-four urban areas attended a Chicago conference on redlining. Within a few years community groups in many cities were rallying around demands for national mandatory disclosure of mortgage lending patterns. They were also pressuring local officials to initiate mortgage reinvestment programs. Out of this growing movement came the idea and the grass-roots pressure behind the Home Mortgage Disclosure Act, enacted in 1975. During the congressional hearings, more than twenty neighborhood organizations from across the country testified, documenting the withdrawal of mortgage money from their communities. Senator William Proxmire of Wisconsin, the author of the bill, acknowledged this unique development after the hearings: "It is hard to recall an issue where impetus for reform came so directly and persuasively from grass roots organizations."[13]

The community and civil rights groups that fought for the disclosure act have become the main organizations using the disclosure data locally to press financial institutions to reinvest in neighborhood housing. In general, government officials concerned with housing have been far slower than the mediating structures to recognize the consequences of redlining and disinvestment and to take the initiative in designing new policies and programs to end this form of discrimination.

In recent years local neighborhood organizations have also become involved in issues related to insurance company policies and insurance rates. Insurance redlining takes various forms, including an automatic blanket denial of insurance coverage to residents of a specific geographic location, extremely high rates, refusal to insure dwellings more than thirty years old, and other policies that make it extremely difficult to get insurance on homes in older neighbor-hoods. In the words of the Michigan Department of Insurance,

> Insurance redlining is particularly severe . . . because the individuals which it victimizes are powerless to reverse it. No amount of home repair or im-provement will make the resident of a redlined neighborhood eligible for homeowner's insurance. Even in the absence of clear-cut redlining, consumers have encountered additional underwriting and application barriers which have the effect of excluding an increasing number of urban residents. Whether subtle or explicit, redlining not only exposes individuals to financial ruin, it also inflicts severe damage upon the entire neighborhood or city involved.[14]

Although neighborhood organizations have taken several approaches to the insurance redlining issues, the overall demand is constant—it is that homeowner's and automobile insurance be available on a nondiscriminatory basis at similar rates throughout metropolitan areas. The work of the United Neighborhood Organization (UNO) in Los Angeles on the insurance redlining issue has been particularly successful. In early 1979, for example, the UNO arranged a meeting between community residents, California Governor Jerry Brown, and executives of twelve major insurance companies to review data used to set the automobile insurance rates in East Los Angeles. Having been called into public accountability in the presence of the state government, the insurers announced a 38 to 43 percent reduction in premiums.

Other groups have taken very different approaches to fair housing issues. Some organizations have created housing referral centers that monitor all property sales in a particular neighborhood. They list local homes for sale, inform buyers of neighborhood trends and the prices of comparable housing, offer counseling to homebuyers, and help new residents adjust to the community. Sellers are given full information on prices and on the availability of conventional as well as FHA and VA financing. The centers take no commissions on sales. In most cases, as Susan Learmonth of Neighbors, Inc., of Washington, D.C., has said, a center's function is "to reassure the whites and make the blacks feel welcome." By acting as a central marketplace to bring together buyer and seller, the referral center is able to bypass the racial steering and selective brokerage listing practices of the real estate firms that specialize in transition. With strong community support, a local housing referral center can gather and disseminate enough information to defuse panic selling and help stabilize an integrated community.

Other groups may not establish a formal structure but use more informal means to strengthen the sense of cohesion within a neighborhood that is undergoing racial transition. Some of these groups function only at the block level, whereas others have a broader neighborhood scope. The usefulness of small, voluntary block clubs in helping create a sense of cohesion in the neighborhood and maintain the quality of housing and public services should not be underestimated.

The Detroit-Edwin-Move (DEM) Street Block Club in Flint, Michigan, provides a typical example of block club activity. Their May 22, 1977, minutes reflect the sense of community engendered by the block club:

> The Block Club decided on petunias to be the club flower. Each member or family of the block club will buy own flowers and set them out as soon as possible. We also decide to have a "Do Your Lawn Day" which would include mowing and improvement of houses. . . . We would like to involve children of families in the block club, especially teenagers. We will try to plan some type of recreation or entertainment for them; example, a weiner roast. We would also like to involve them in having pride and helping take care of their home and lawns, and possibly form a junior block club. . . . We gave the school part of the proceeds made from the Bunche Fair bake sale and guess your weight game, amounting to $26.10.[15]

DEM's accomplishments include the following:

- Getting the city to demolish a badly deteriorated vacant home in their area;
- Building a sense of community pride and involvement and bringing elderly residents into the mainstream of community life (there is a senior citizens' home in the area, and block club members extend dinner invitations to the seniors on holidays);
- Securing more adequate trash collection services;
- Establishing a neighbors' watch effort as a crime deterrent;
- Sponsoring periodic neighborhood cleanup campaigns.

DEM is beginning to examine broader issues and problems in neighborhood preservation of their community and in the city as a whole. The group is considering involvement in more demanding, long-range projects, such as the purchase and rehabilitation of an area home, employment of youth in neighborhood improvement projects, and a detailed examination of the redlining problem in their community. Club members are also concerned about plans for the use and development of vacant lots in the neighborhood. DEM provides an excellent example of how block-level initiatives toward neighborhood beautification can serve as a catalyst for involvement in the more complex issues of planning and development for neighborhood preservation.

SUPPORT FOR REFORMS
IN HOUSING POLICY

Mediating structures have also played a leading role in seeking reforms in the policies of both private and public institutions relating to transitional neighborhoods. The main impetus for many of the reforms that have gradually been introduced in FHA programs since the early 1970s has come from neighborhood groups. Chicago's Metropolitan Area Housing Alliance (MAHA) and its forerunners have been particularly active. In 1973, its first year of operation, MAHA accomplished the following:

- Persuaded the FHA not to issue mortgage insurance without a certificate from the Chicago Building Department stating that the home had been inspected and found free of code violations;
- Persuaded the FHA to stop hiring fee appraisers and to require that their own staff appraise each insured house, thus increasing supervision and reducing the opportunity for fraudulent over-appraisals and kickbacks;
- Persuaded the FHA to create an office of follow-up counseling to help buyers of FHA-insured homes that had major structural defects;
- Through testimony at Senate hearings in Chicago, pressed successfully for federal legislation to reimburse FHA homebuyers for the cost of remedying such structural defects.

Legislation enacted in 1975 in Illinois to begin state regulation of mortgage bankers resulted from an initiative taken by neighborhood organizations working in coalition to obtain support from the governor and the state legislature. The temporary suspension by the FHA of the Advance Mortgage Company, the nation's largest mortgage banking firm, resulted from complaints by community groups throughout the country. Congressional hearing records provide example after example of reform initiatives from various kinds of community organizations, including church-based groups and other voluntary associations.

Community groups have also taken the lead in successful efforts to legislate mandatory reimbursement to homebuyers buying FHA-insured homes with serious structural defects that endanger health and safety. In addition to the limited 518 (b) reimbursement program already introduced, these groups have pressed for a permanent warranty program on all FHA-insured homes.

Some neighborhood organizations' reform efforts have been directed at local government agencies rather than at federal agencies or private institutions. Community groups in low- and moderate-income neighborhoods in virtually every city have vociferously argued for increased public services and public investment in their communities. They have asked for more policemen, better garbage pickup and street maintenance, the retention of fire stations and other facilities, and the investment of city-controlled housing and Community Development Block Grant funds in their neighborhoods.

This battle has occasionally surfaced at the national level. In 1977 and 1978, neighborhood groups joined with church-related organizations, civil rights groups, and public interest organizations in a national battle over the allocation of $3.5 billion in federal Community Development Block Grant programs. They lobbied with some success for a greater allocation of these block grant funds to low- and moderate-income neighborhoods, demanding that a full 75 percent of the money be spent in such areas.

At the local level, such groups have fought to have their neighborhoods designated for concentrations of block grant funds and to have larger amounts of the funds spent on housing rehabilitation and other housing needs, rather than on government administrative costs or downtown redevelopment projects.

CREATION OF NEW SERVICES
AND ALTERNATIVE INSTITUTIONS

Finally, local citizens have created a number of organizations and services designed to meet needs not met by large outside private and public institutions. With remarkable vitality and creativity, local citizens have established impressive programs to meet local needs. Among these are the following:

- Prepurchase counseling services to help potential homebuyers budget to meet housing expenses and learn to inspect and evaluate a house before deciding to buy;
- Default and delinquency counseling programs to help homeowners meet the crisis created when they miss mortgage payments and to advise them on the best course of action and on their rights;
- Cooperative home maintenance and repair services, which allow a homeowner to pay a set amount per year in exchange for specified repair and maintenance services;
- Neighborhood Housing Services programs, which bring together community residents, private lenders, and government officials in a joint project to stimulate greater reinvestment, improved public services, and increased rehabilitation activity.

The Neighborhood Housing Services (NHS) program (see Chapter 2) illustrates the promise of a mediating structures approach. It emphasizes the importance of process and of involving local people in negotiations with megastructures on policies affecting their lives.

One of the keys to the NHS success has been its process. By involving community, financial, and local government representatives in an ongoing relationship, most NHS programs have gradually strengthened cooperation among the three groups with the greatest influence over a community's future. In many cases there have been important changes in attitudes as people have learned more about one another's concerns and perspectives. NHS leaders are especially enthusiastic about changes the NHS process has brought to the attitudes of financial institutions that, through direct involvement in the neighborhood and growing confidence in the community and local government commitment to the area, have been reassured about the future of neighborhoods formerly written off and redlined.

Two factors have been especially important to the success of the NHS program. First, it was developed to respond to the needs of each particular neighborhood, as defined by the neighborhood's residents and by the financial and public institutions closest to the community. Second, it spread gradually, neighborhood by neighborhood, adapting to variations in local conditions and always involving the private, public, and community sectors. This history and this success are in notable contrast to the usual megastructure program—created by outsiders and imposed on a wholesale basis with minimum involvement of local citizens and virtually no attention to the goals of bringing change to attitudes and institutions.

PUBLIC POLICY IMPLICATIONS

Over the past four decades, federal housing policy has generally ignored most of the issues raised in this discussion of transitional neighborhoods. Although debate has raged periodically on such issues as the level of federal subsidies for housing, the degree of federal control over local housing programing, and the mix of program approaches, HUD has done little to examine the roles and performance of various types of institutions, whether megastructures or mediating structures. It has been almost equally neglectful of the effect of present policies on those institutions, especially on the health and vitality of neighborhoods and mediating structures.

Although a dozen years have passed since Congress enacted Title VIII of the Civil Rights Act of 1968, which gave HUD the means to become involved in eliminating racial steering, block-busting, and other discriminatory real estate practices, HUD has not yet issued regulations to guide the courts and others in applying the civil rights protections to housing. Nor has HUD conducted a major study of the issues raised in this discussion and in congressional testimony by church and neighborhood leaders concerning the mortgage banking industry, which developed as a byproduct of federal programs. The department has also been slow to deal with redlining. Before 1979 it conducted little research on this issue, and it has generally been unimaginative in viewing the part it could play in helping eliminate disinvestment by means of demonstration grants, technical assistance to local governments and neighborhood groups, and other uses of its resources and leadership.

HUD has been loath to examine the potential for expanding the roles of mediating structures in federal policy. It has generally found distasteful the forceful criticism of HUD policies that has come from neighborhood, church, civil rights, and public interest groups. It has seldom viewed the criticism as helpful to the department. The department has stubbornly resisted any expansion of resources available to neighborhood groups and other mediating structures that are delivering important services and contributing substantially to local community development efforts. The fight over funding for counseling agencies has raged for a decade, with HUD opposing major funding until recently, largely because of concern that counseling agencies often act as advocates for home-owners and seek broad reforms in the operation of FHA programs. After many years of providing no support at all for such groups, HUD in 1978 began allocating funds for a limited number of neigh-borhood development organizations. However, HUD yielded to pressure from local officials and barred grants to community groups without the concurrence of local public officials. This ensured that many of the most constructive community groups were effectively blocked from receiving direct HUD support because local officials opposed public support of such private initiatives. In a letter to HUD, the executive director of the U.S. Conference of Mayors attacked funding for community groups even with a consent re-quirement. Apparently advancing the notion that local governments should have a monopoly of all public resources, the executive direc-tor, John Gunther, wrote:

> there is a deep concern among the Mayors that the Administration continues to indicate that it wants to help cities but intends to do this by . . . directly funding community groups. Frankly, the Mayors are very puzzled that there seems to be a lack of helping cities by helping cities. As indicated in our discussions, this is not a nation of federal neighborhoods but of local neigh-borhoods and communities.
>
> We believe that neighborhood achievement can best be made by the neighborhoods in close cooperation with their fellow neighborhoods and their city government. Direct federal funding of community or neighbor-hoods does not appear to be a move to bring about progress or harmony in cities.[16]

By making these small resources subject to local government control, effectively adding them to the tens of billions of dollars already flowing to local governments, the nation is giving local officials a stranglehold on all public resources designed to solve neighborhood problems. This monopoly eliminates the chance to capitalize on the pluralism, the variety of approaches, America has historically under-taken in seeking answers to problems. Such a narrow, centralized approach constrains creativity and is especially inimical to neighborhood revitalization, which requires unusually diverse and sensitive new approaches. It is vital to encourage neighborhood organizations, which have demonstrated that they can develop sound approaches to redlining, reinvestment, crime, rehabilitation, housing management, and decentralized social services. They need resources so that they can experiment with new approaches, some of which may—because they are unconventional or especially promising—threaten less creative, less dynamic, entrenched public and private agencies.

To foster creative neighborhood groups and mediating structures, federal programs should provide direct financial support when needed. Most neighborhood organizations have such limited financial and technical resources that they are not able to participate as equal partners with major public and private institutions. If mediating structures are to function effectively and become full partners, they must be given direct, unencumbered access to resources that will allow them to develop their programmatic knowledge, technical capacity, and strength.

REFERENCES

1. Gregory Gordon and Albert Swanson, *Chicago: Evaluation of a Ghetto* (Chicago: Leadership Council on Metropolitan Opportunity, 1977), p. 8.

2. Ibid., pp. 11–12.

3. Ibid., p. 6.

4. Ibid., p. 16.

5. Saul B. Klaman, *The Postwar Rise of Mortgage Companies,* National Bureau of Economic Research Occasional Paper) #100-60 (National Bureau of Economic Research, 1976), p. 166.

6. Philip Edwin Kidd, *Mortgage Banking 1963-1972, (Ph.D. diss., American University,* 1976), p. 166.

7. U.S. Congress, House, H.R. Report No. 20, *Reducing Losses through Improved Mortgage Servicing,* 94th Congress, 2d sess., March 29, 1976, p. 7.

8. Center for Community Change, *Opportunities for Abuse: Private Profits, Public Losses, and the Mortgage Banking Industry* (Washington, 1977).

9. Author interview with Gale Cincotta, February 9, 1978.

10. Center for Community Change and Center for National Policy Review, *Neighborhood Conservation and Housing Opportunity: How Do We Avoid another Marquette Park?* (Report prepared for U.S. Department of Housing and Urban Development, 1977), p. 3.

11. Jane Jacobs, *The Death and Life of Great American Cities* (New York: Random House, 1961).

12. U.S. Commission on Civil Rights, *Report 4-Housing* (Washington, 1978), p. 29.

13. Arthur Naparstek and Gale Cincotta, *Urban Disinvestment: New Implications for Community Organizations, Research and Public Policy* (National Center for Urban Ethnic Affairs, 1978), p. 5.

14. State of Michigan Insurance Department, *Essential Insurance in Michigan: An Avoidable Crisis* (Lansing, Mich., 1977).

15. Detroit-Edwin-Move Block Club, *Minutes* (Flint, Mich., May 22, 1977).

16. John Gunther, *Correspondence with Department of H.U.D.*, February 1978.

5 SUBURBAN INTEGRATION

Mary and Jim, a young, middle-class black couple with two children, wanted to move from their city apartment to a residential suburb. Their neighborhood was deteriorating rapidly. Mary and Jim visited five suburbs in different parts of the area. In all of them they were told by real estate agents that no homes were available. Finally, a real estate agent steered them to an older suburb and sold them a house at what turned out to be an inflated price. Within a year, as a result of blockbusting and scare tactics, 80 percent of the original residents had moved out, deterioration had set in, and Mary and Jim began making plans to move again.

Mary and Jim, though fictional, represent a reality encountered in city after city in America. Their story illustrates the patterns described in Chapters 3 and 4. Families find inner city and transitional neighborhoods failing. Disruption and neglect of mediating structures accelerate the flow of the more affluent to the suburbs. Jim and Mary were frustrated initially because they wanted to stay in a functioning urban neighborhood. Once they made the decision to move, a decision based on class lines, they were frustrated by the widespread illegal discrimination and inadequate enforcement of civil rights laws. Finally, when they obtained a home in a middle-class area, their dream evaporated because of panic and the unethical tactics of real estate and financial institutions.

Just as in transitional urban neighborhoods, fear is a dominant element in the integration of suburban areas. The fear is in some cases based on plain prejudice. In other cases, it is based on a more complex set of attitudes about class—a fear that new residents will not have the inclination or means to maintain either property or the neighborhood ethos. Ironically, the desire for suburban housing on the part of middle-class people such as Mary and Jim reflects an appreciation of the ethos they are seen as threatening.

Some fears of integration are based on mistaken views of federal policy. For example, many suburbs fear that massive government-subsidized public housing will come to their areas. In fact, this kind of dispersal policy has never been seriously embraced by Congress or either major political party. The prospects of this or any other government-mandated dispersal policy are next to zero over the next eight years. The Arlington Heights ruling—suburban zoning can be stricken down as exclusionary *only* if intent is proved—had the effect of severely limiting any judicial remedies against suburban restrictiveness. Similarly, present HUD policies, with stringent congressional oversight, make it virtually impossible to build public housing outside central city political boundaries.

And yet, though often factually unfounded, fears touching race and class issues become causes of suburban destabilization. Fearful residents become easy prey for predatory megastructures. Panic sets in. Original homeowners and new ones such as Mary and Jim flee, and the area quickly fills with lower income families. Absentee ownership increases, and panic spreads.

Fear is further magnified by the funneling effect that occurs in metropolitan areas. Because the vast majority of suburbs oppose any kind of change, change tends to be funneled into one area at a time. Like Mary and Jim, initial urban emigrés find doors shut until they are steered to one area. Then unscrupulous real estate brokers tend to exploit the situation, and destabilization occurs.

Government has been remarkably unsuccessful in aiding the process of voluntary integration. Civil rights laws in the area of housing are seldom enforced. And government's failure to meet the needs of inner city and transitional neighborhoods means that people whose first choice is to stay in their urban neighborhoods are pushed into the stream of suburban migration.

Mediating structures in the past have played a significant role in helping individuals cope with these problems so that they can choose out of confidence rather than fear. The case of Oak Park, Illinois, is instructive.

OAK PARK

Oak Park is a small older suburb (some 70,000 people) on the western edge of Chicago. An area of substantial homes, it developed as a quiet, peaceful place for middle- to upper-middle-class professional and white-collar workers. Oak Park in 1960 was 99 percent white.

In many ways, though incorporated as a village, Oak Park is a neighborhood. There is little industry, and a majority of its residents work in Chicago. Oak Park, although not identified with one specific ethnic group, nevertheless has a very strong ethos, family oriented with a tradition of high-quality education, public and private. Great stress is placed on neatness and cleanliness. Property is well kept, and property values were stable or rising in the 1960s.

At the same time that Oak Park flourished, the grim realities of Chicago's neighborhood destabilization spread westward from the Loop, neighborhood by neighborhood. In the late 1960s, the integration of Austin, just to the east of Oak Park, began with great conflict and animosity. Racial change brought "panic peddlers" and blockbusters. In the words of Gale Cincotta, then head of the Organization for a Better Austin and later a national housing leader, "The suede shoe artists came in, buying shoddy homes, painting them, and selling them at profits of $10,000 or $15,000." Austin, in short, was going through the process that later engulfed Marquette Park.

When neighborhoods such as Austin begin to change, an immediate fear is that the "others" coming in will destroy the values and way of life of the community. Old residents fear that new neighbors will not maintain their property or that building codes will not be enforced, introducing multiple dwellings, deterioration of properties, and increased noise. They fear crime, the decline of city services, and diminished political power. They also fear a shortage of mortgage money for rehabilitation and purchases.

Robert Bailey, in his book *Radicals in Urban Politics,* vividly portrays this process. Referring to Austin in 1969, after rapid social change had occurred, he wrote:

Eighty-three percent of South Austin residents have moved into the community within the past five years, 58 percent within the past two years. The newcomers are blacks, who entered as the whites fled. During twenty-six months of fieldwork, one square mile of South Austin changed from white to black. Seventy-six percent of the local population is black, and 21 percent is white.[1]

As resegregation occurred, the established Protestant churches usually disbanded or severely curtailed operations. The comments of a Presbyterian minister indicate the problems of the church and its white parishioners in a changing neighborhood:

Four years ago I had about 700 members and I brought in 287, but 600 other members moved out. There are no kids in Sunday school, there were 250. Today, out of 365 members, 212 are widows. There are only three families left with children. The whites who are left are trapped, generally the elderly; we have school, housing and violence problems. Now in the neighborhood alcoholism is on the upswing. Often many families are now living in what was before a single-family home.[2]

The visible reminders of crime, jimmied mailboxes, and jarred door latches, were ever present in South Austin. A few policemen coped with the problem by telling residents to "move to a safer area" or to "buy yourself a bat."[3]

The quotations are not intended to portray the full reality of Austin. They simply show the perceptions and fears of the residents. These became the perceptions and fears of the residents of Oak Park in the late 1960s. Yet Oak Park was to become one of the more successful examples of racial integration (not, class integration, however; this discussion limits itself primarily to the issue of racial integration.)

In 1969 it was being confidently said that by 1980 Oak Park would have gone the way of Austin. Some predicted that Oak Park would be 25 percent black by 1975 and 50 percent by 1980.[a] It was expected that the introduction of racial change would cause the classic pattern—flight of whites, temporarily depressed values, speculative exploitation, disinvestment, and the tragic loss of most community institutions.

Oak Park first attempted to resist integration altogether. After passage of an open housing ordinance in 1968, a town board election became a bitter referendum on whether to continue to strive for

a. It should be stressed emphatically here that we are not saying that a 50 percent black neighborhood is bad. We use this statistic in a practical context; that is, when integration is introduced in Chicago suburbs, it tends to cause panicked flight and destruction of neighborhood institutions. The effect is resegregation, with few community institutions left to mediate the effects of rapid change.

antidiscrimination measures. A prointegration group headed by the board president, Jack Gearen, won but faced the problem of how to eliminate discrimination and, at the same time, convince old residents that the socioeconomic character of the city would not change dramatically.

A series of actions, all initiated locally, succeeded in opening Oak Park to all races while retaining its ambience as a middle-class suburb. These positive initiatives were rooted in, and in certain crucial cases directed by, mediating structures, especially block clubs and neighborhood organizations. Two deserve special attention: the Housing Center and the Community Relations Department.

THE HOUSING CENTER

The Housing Center started in 1972 under the guidance of a young woman, Bobby Raymond, who was committed to integration in every respect. She realized that most integration attempts failed and that much racial animosity was rooted in fears of changes in neighborhood class structure. She also realized that if Oak Park went through the traditional cycle of integration, resegregation, and decay, everyone would lose.

The Housing Center developed a variety of programs aimed at stabilizing community expectations about the future. It first organized block clubs. The aim was to communicate accurate information as quickly as possible. Out of the rumor-squelching stage grew a two-way system of communication, from the center to the block clubs and from the clubs back to the center.

Raymond and her co-workers embarked on a controversial strategy. In effect they said that in the transition blacks should distribute themselves throughout Oak Park so as to avoid threatening concentrations. A process of reverse steering began. Black families were counseled about the various neighborhoods of Oak Park and steered, in many cases, to wholly white areas so as to avoid resegregation. In an allied move, the coalition around the Housing Center got a local ordinance passed forbidding For Sale signs in yards, these often being used by real estate agents to induce panic selling. In some cases, the real estate brokers were bypassed altogether, the center itself purchasing homes and then reselling them.

Support for this mediating structure came from other groups.

A grant for initial costs and space for the Housing Center came from the First Congregational Church (later merged with the First Presbyterian Church to become the First United Church). The leaders in retrospect comment strikingly on the role of volunteers from church and neighborhood groups. Ms. Raymond estimates that several million dollars of volunteer time have been expended in the program since 1971. Along with housing counseling, the center lobbied for code enforcement, hoping to ensure basic stability of expectations on the part of all residents. Information programs staffed by volunteers were begun in the schools.

The magnitude of the effort is reflected in some of the statistics. For example, from May 1976 to April 1977, the Housing Center served 5,461 clients in its rental referral program alone. This involved counseling, referral, and in some cases the controversial reverse steering to avoid resegregation. It rehabilitated an apartment building and sold it to a private investor. It engaged in an extensive public relations campaign that aggressively marketed Oak Park as an attractive place to live and maintained a program of communications with real estate agents and apartment owners, enlisting their cooperation. Cited in several national publications for the intensity of its efforts, the Housing Center nevertheless had a budget of only $58,000 in 1976, much of it raised from private sources.[5]

THE COMMUNITY RELATIONS DEPARTMENT

The Community Relations Department works under the direction of citizen members of the Human Relations Commission created by the village in 1963. The department has five major tasks:

- Education and consultation
- Investigation of complaints and rumors
- Block area organizing
- Diversity counseling
- Affirmative marketing

Under the direction of community organizer Kris Ronnow, the department sponsored 173 block parties in 1976 and organized more than 300 block clubs funded by the municipality.

Megastructures, particularly some real estate agents and apartment speculators, presented major obstacles to the department's work. In one year, for example, the Human Relations Commission received more than 2,700 calls related to real estate practices. Most of the complaints were settled informally, but in 1976, thirty-nine cases reached the formal complaint adjudication process. Kris Ronnow has estimated that the department was responsible for the revocation of fifteen to twenty real estate brokerage licenses during an eight-year period.

Some important factors in the Oak Park story:

- Oak Park had forceful leadership in both public and private sectors during its crisis.
- The interest in historic preservation made the Frank Lloyd Wright architecture in the community a major asset for attracting upper-middle-income families.
- In 1971 and 1972, and again more recently, high interest rates generally reduced mobility, and Oak Park residents were less likely to move.
- Community organizing efforts in Austin helped make Austin more attractive and reduced the flight to Oak Park.
- Physical improvements, such as the renovation of the shopping area into the Oak Park Mall, helped restore confidence.
- The city initiated major programs to restore confidence, including systematic code enforcement and an experimental Housing Equity Assurance program that protected homebuyers from possible depreciation in housing values.

Almost every observer agrees that the grass-roots organizations, the Housing Center, and the citizen-oriented Human Relations Commission made indispensable contributions to the community's preservation and integration.

Oak Park has achieved what few communities in the nation have—integration with real equality of opportunity in housing without the cycle of panic, disinvestment, and resegregation. At present, Oak Park has approximately 10 percent minority residents. Elementary schools have approximately 20 percent minority enrollment. Housing values have soared. Homes in many areas have doubled and tripled in value since 1971. Oak Park still faces problems, but community confidence is strong.

ANALYSIS

First, what happened in Oak Park came almost wholly as a result of initiatives of local residents.

Second, what we call mediating structures were crucial in devising and implementing the programs in Oak Park. Both formally and informally, the web of community relations was indispensable in achieving goals.

Third, when mobilized for positive action, the energies of citizens far outweighed any possible monetary support by the federal or state government. Bobby Raymond estimated the volunteer time in the millions of dollars. Added to this must be the greater amount of time spent improving and maintaining property. Disinvestment is not only institutional but personal. The normal yearly maintenance involved in keeping a property attractive amounts to close to $2,000 (painting, lawn work, small repairs, gutters, trash cleanup, and so on). Because Oak Park was able to maintain confidence in the community, these indispensable resources continued to be invested in the community.

Fourth, Oak Park had some advantages over communities like Austin and Marquette Park. It had higher incomes, more professionals in its population, and a more exclusive housing market to begin with. Oak Park had greater stability and greater resources with which to mediate change. It is clear that the communities least able to accommodate socioeconomic change are those with the least resources. What are called second-tier neighborhoods, blue-collar, working-class areas, are most fragile. To the extent that communities like Oak Park pursue positive programs, pressure is taken off nearby communities.

Fifth, the process of integration, resegregation, and decay neighborhood by neighborhood goes on both because of a shortage of success stories, such as Oak Park, and because central core neighborhoods continue to disintegrate. Any sensible strategy must provide opportunities for residents of central city neighborhoods to revitalize their own communities, as well as open a variety of discrimination-free opportunities if they choose to move.

Sixth, the reverse steering, whereby blacks are encouraged to disperse throughout the village rather than concentrate in clusters, was probably important to the success of the Housing Center and the Community Relations Department. The policy was officially adopted by the board of trustees and the village president in 1973 and was unanimously reaffirmed in 1977. The resolution, entitled "Maintaining Diversity in Oak Park," reads in part: "A free and open community—equal and diverse—can only be achieved through dispersal; a mixture of racial and ethnic groups throughout the Village."

Some black leaders have objected to such policies. Certainly dangers exist in dispersal. Such a program could be a charade for discrimination. But it is important to note several factors:

- The policy did not arise in a vacuum. It was devised to counter a prior trend—the large-scale racial steering practiced by some real estate interests. If the first kind of steering can be eliminated, reverse steering may not be necessary.
- Evidence indicates that both black and white residents were enabled to achieve their goal—a middle-class residential ethos. It was not that blacks wanted an all-black area in Oak Park. They wanted a property, a high-quality, school-oriented suburb. Reverse steering, by preventing panic and the advent of speculators, allowed them to achieve their goals.
- As racism declines, the need for such programs will recede. If the tragic link in some people's minds between race and class can be broken, truly free choices for individuals can emerge. Most residents in Oak Park feared *low-income* blacks changing the class ethos of the community. Reverse steering, at least in the interim, neutralizes predatory megastructures and demonstrates that race has nothing to do with class.

Oak Park has achieved what few communities in this country have, a truly integrated housing market without racial discrimination. It has also clearly maintained a socioeconomic self-definition. Property codes, ordinances, cleanup programs—all of these have maintained an ethos long characteristic of Oak Park. One does not have to embrace Oak Park's values to see the practical lesson: that in achieving equality of opportunity, one must allow space for preserving choices in life-style within neighborhoods.

This chapter leaves the practical questions unanswered. Our final chapters, dealing with strategies and policies, address the concrete implications of our analysis.

REFERENCES

1. Robert Bailey, *Radicals in Urban Politics* (Chicago: University of Chicago Press, 1974), p. 7.
2. Ibid., p. 8.
3. Ibid., p. 11.
4. Oak Park Housing Center, *Annual Reports 1976 and 1977* (Oak Park, Illinois).

6 THE DILEMMAS OF INNER CITY REVITALIZATION

The inner cities of America are poised for a stunning comeback, a turnabout in their fortunes that could be one of the most significant developments in our national history.

Neal R. Peirce
Nation's Cities, March 1978

"They're coming back" trumpets the brochure describing the Asylum Hill neighborhood of Hartford. Handsome pictures of young, affluent-looking whites and blacks with tennis rackets project a new image for a community adjacent to the headquarters of several of America's largest insurance companies. The area, which was wealthy until two or three decades ago, went through a long period of racial and economic transition, and is now beginning to be "rediscovered" again.

The realtor's description of the neighborhood is inscribed on paper which resembles parchment. "This community of stately Victorian homes with elegant fireplaces, fine woodwork, and elegant detailing offers outstanding values for families seeking investment opportunities in the city." Quite clearly, Washington's Mount Pleasant neighborhood—which has in recent years been 70–80% minority—is changing rapidly and will soon follow Capitol Hill, Adams Morgan, and other neighborhoods and become a predominantly white, upper middle class community.

The real question is who cities will be saved for: the big corporations and the returning middle class, or for the poor, the jobless, the people who always seem to be shortchanged by our society? Are cities collections of skyscrapers, or groups of human beings? Who will cities be saved for?

Nicholas Carbone
Hartford City Council
Harper's Magazine, December 1978

Something new is happening in American cities. Even as the Carter administration's urban policy stagnated on Capitol Hill, the cities were starting to attract and keep a new generation of people. This essentially private market phenomenon is still in its infancy, but it raises significant questions about the future of inner city housing. The surprising fact is that some neighborhoods that had been declining for years began to experience an infusion of new investment and life. In most of our major cities, there are one or more neighborhoods renewing their housing stock, recovering a sense of confidence and momentum, and attracting new people and resources.

This new activity is not a simple phenomenon. It is a double-edged sword. In some cases this revitalization has been good for the city, the neighborhoods, and the people in them. However, in a significant number of neighborhoods, this revitalization has cost minority and poor residents their homes and their community ties. They have been displaced by new, and more affluent households that can compete more effectively for the amenities of central city life.

Inner city revitalization is clearly happening; less clear is whether it will contribute to the easing of housing and urban problems or simply shift them to neighborhoods less attractive to the new urbanites. Revitalization that ignores the people and existing mediating structures in urban neighborhoods will not bring the "rebirth of our cities" but, rather, new class and racial conflict. Far from saving our cities, such a process would make urban life a high-stakes game of "musical chairs." Current objections to the displacement often caused by revitalization show that it may touch off a divisive struggle over "turf" and further aggravate relations between people of different races and incomes.

We are convinced that a key factor in determining whether the forces of revitalization are harnessed to work in the interests of neighborhood residents or will work against and overwhelm those interests will be the strength, skill, and sophistication of the local mediating structures. Those neighborhoods that are well organized and that have community associations determined to help shape and manage reinvestment may prosper. Neighborhoods without such structures, or in which mediating structures are so weak that they are displaced along with the earlier residents, will be unable to protect their people from the sometimes brutal social forces of what the British call "gentrification."

THE DIMENSIONS OF REVITALIZATION

The process of revitalization is not confined to a few cities. It extends far beyond Washington's Georgetown and Capitol Hill. A 1975 study by the Urban Land Institute indicated that neighborhood revitalization was occurring in almost half of cities with more than 50,000 people and 75 percent of cities with populations greater than 500,000.[1] Nathaniel Rogg, in a study for the U.S. League of Savings and Loan Associations, says that virtually every large city is experiencing some revitalization.[2] Robert Franklin, in a HUD-sponsored survey, discovered a surprising reversal of housing and investment trends in the mid-1970s.[3] He found that between 1973 and 1975 property values increased slightly faster in central cities than in suburbs, a sharp reversal of historical trends. And central city homeowners spent more than suburban homeowners for home improvements during the same period. There has been a small but significant increase in homeownership in central cities; it is estimated that owner-occupied housing units in cities increased by 170,000 between 1970 and 1975.

This phenomenon should not be mistaken for a broad-scale urban recovery. More people continue to move out of the cities than move in. Even Washington, D.C., which is experiencing the greatest degree of revitalization, is still losing population. Many neighborhoods and cities continue to experience disinvestment by financial institutions. Many cities continue to lose people, especially affluent and working-class families. Between 1970 and 1974, incomes of people moving into the city averaged $1,305 less than incomes of those moving out. Urban property tax revenues are still declining, and cities are left to fight worsening problems with fewer resources. Cleveland, Newark, New York, and other cities still face grim futures. For every neighborhood revitalized in the past few years, there have been many others that have slipped deeper and deeper into decline. For every family displaced by reinvestment, far more have been displaced by the consequences of disinvestment. Revitalization is estimated to affect fewer than 5 percent of all urban housing units, perhaps no more than 2 percent of inner city housing stock. However, these percentages may grow, and they do constitute a glimmer of hope in the midst of gloom.

CAUSES

The possible causes of this revival of interest in central city housing and neighborhoods include changed economic realities, new social forces, and a number of physical factors.

The economic and demographic trends of the mid-1970s combined to make inner-urban housing an attractive economic alternative to suburban homes. Between 1963 and 1978, the median cost of a new home rose from under $20,000 to over $57,000; property taxes more than doubled between 1967 and 1975. This meant that the suburban dream house was beyond the reach for many young families. The mid–1970s also saw housing production fall dramatically as a result of the Nixon administration's housing policies and an economic recession. Housing production fell far short of meeting the needs of new households in 1974, 1975, and 1976. The number of those seeking housing was swelled by the maturation of those born during the post–World War II baby boom. Young adults left their dormitories or parents' homes to pursue their careers, start families, and find apartments or purchase homes. The combination of rising costs, low housing production in the suburbs, and growing need produced new pressure on an old resource—inner city housing.

Unlike the suburbs, where high demand was bidding up the costs of housing, central city disinvestment, decay, and inflation led to depressed prices for housing and to actual abandonment. Houses could be purchased and rehabilitated for 50 to 60 percent of the cost of building a new home.

A number of economic and geographic realities strengthened the city's ability to attract these new households. The oil embargo of 1974 and rising energy prices brought home to many Americans the high cost of commuting long distances to work. The suburbs suddenly seemed less attractive.

At the same time, cities had substantial physical assets, one of them being existing housing. This housing varied enormously, but it included some homes of architectural significance and neighborhoods of historical interest. Many cities had homes originally constructed for affluent residents, with features not available in suburban subdivisions. City neighborhoods had the advantage of proximity to culture and entertainment and, in some cases, to mass transit. Cities were also attempting to revive their downtowns. Quincy Market in Boston, the Waterfront in Baltimore, the Underground in Atlanta, the Gateway Project in Minneapolis, the Kennedy Center in Washington are examples of such efforts. Many of these are the legacy of the urban renewal program of the 1950s and 1960s and other massive public investments.

Social changes contributed to making inner city housing attractive. Family life was assuming new forms as couples pursued two careers (often both downtown) and postponed children. Schools became less important in housing choices than access to employment and entertainment. A new generation paused before leaving their urban apartments for the suburban subdivisions.

Finally, and somewhat ironically, the neighborhood organizations that had emerged to fight for the interests of those who had stayed in the inner city contributed to the desirability of older neighborhoods. In pursuing improvements that would help current residents, they helped attract new people who would often wind up displacing the constituency of the neighborhood groups. In blocking freeways and renewal projects that disrupted communities, in pressing financial institutions to reinvest in redlined areas, in tackling crime, deteriorating schools, and unresponsive city governments, and in creating a sense of appreciation for ethnic and community roots, neighborhood groups helped create the preconditions for attracting middle-class people to the community.

GENTRIFICATION VERSUS UPGRADING

In one of the most extensive studies of urban revitalization, Phillip Clay of the Massachusetts Institute of Technology analyzed 105 neighborhoods in the thirty largest cities.[4] He concluded that two very different types of revitalization were under way. The first was gentrification, a process of private rehabilitation by predominantly white, affluent professionals from outside the neighborhood. This process frequently resulted in substantially higher prices, significant displacement, and major change in neighborhood characteristics.

The second form of revitalization Clay calls "incumbent upgrading." This is a process of rehabilitation and renewal in moderate-income areas carried on for the most part by present residents. Its consequences appear to be far less destructive of the neighborhood's fabric.

For our purposes, the most significant difference between the two forms of revitalization is the role of mediating structures. In gentrification areas, neighborhood or community organizations played almost no part in initiating or sustaining rehabilitation. The renewal of the area was essentially undertaken by individual pioneers and developers. In contrast, neighborhood organizations were a major factor throughout the revitalization process in upgrading areas. Neighborhood initiatives played a key role in less than 4 percent of the gentrification areas, but organized neighborhood efforts or public efforts (often the result of community pressure) were the first signs of revitalization in almost half (47 percent) of the upgrading areas.

The Clay study found other significant and perhaps related differences between the two types of revitalization. Gentrification appeared to dominate in older, less stable, more decaying areas close to central business districts or specific geographical attractions (rivers, hills, etc.). They also tended to be smaller areas with large populations of elderly, minority, or low-income residents (those least likely to be able to defend their interests). Of twenty-seven areas that were predominantly black before gentrification, well over half (seventeen) were predominantly white when Clay surveyed them. In 70 percent of the gentrification areas, Clay found that revitalization activity was generated mainly by outsiders.

In contrast, renovation in upgrading neighborhoods was carried out for the most part by existing residents and some newcomers of similar socioeconomic class. These neighborhoods appeared to be larger than gentrifying areas, and rehabilitation tended to be more widespread. Less than one-fourth of the upgrading neighborhoods were found to rely mainly on outsiders for rehabilitation activity.

The Upgrading Process

As earlier chapters have shown, various kinds of mediating structures have assisted efforts to arrest decline and to upgrade neighborhoods. The spontaneous growth of block clubs; the paint-up, fix-up campaigns of churches; the banding together of tough, angry community groups to fight urban renewal or declining services or redlining; the development of substantial self-help and development programs by various types of nonprofit organizations—all these efforts contribute to the upgrading of a neighborhood, and all are aimed at ensuring that current residents are the principal beneficiaries of the improvements.

In many communities, mediating structures actually undertake programs of rehabilitation and maintenance. Renew, Inc., of South Bend, Indiana, has established a program whereby local church groups buy homes and rehabilitate them. Potential homeowners receive housing counseling and accumulate sweat equity down payments by their volunteer work in the rehabilitation process. Renew has restored more than sixty homes in a six-year period.

In St. Paul, Minnesota, the Lexington Hamline Community Association has begun a program of cooperative housing maintenance, encouraging maintenance efforts through cooperative agreements between the association and service contractors. Discussions have been held on cooperative and condominium upkeep as a model for urban neighborhoods.

The Woodlawn Organization (TWO) in Chicago and its subsidiary, the Woodlawn Community Development Corporation, have been widely recognized for their work on upgrading a poor black neighborhood. Moving "from protest to program," from confrontation to development, TWO has in recent years developed more than 900 housing units, many designed to attract middle-income people back to Woodlawn on terms that are not only acceptable but advantageous to current Woodlawn residents. In developing the 322-apartment Jackson Park Terrace project, for example, TWO set out to house both poor people and people of moderate and middle income in a stable, high-quality, integrated environment. Jackson Park Terrace has achieved this goal: its tenancy is a mixture of incomes, and it furnishes a model for other TWO projects.

In more than fifty cities, mediating structures are involved in a partnership with government and financial institutions to upgrade neighborhoods through the Neighborhood Housing Services program of the federal Urban Reinvestment Task Force. It is no coincidence that this is by far the most successful and widely hailed urban initiative of the federal government. As noted in Chapter 4, NHS works in neighborhoods with high levels of ownership and basically sound housing stock beginning to deteriorate.

The Gentrification Process

The gentrification process, as described by Rolf Goetze, a housing specialist with the city of Boston, follows a series of stages that resemble the stages of classical American pioneering.[5] First, a small group of "urban pioneers" willing to take economic risks move into a poor neighborhood, purchase old houses, and begin renovation. This group is followed by a larger number of "early settlers" willing to take somewhat lesser risks to gain the convenience and potential economic and cultural advantages of city life. When these early efforts are reported by real estate firms, the media, or the residents themselves, a larger group becomes intensely interested in the neighborhood and creates a boom town psychology, with rapidly rising prices and competition for homes in the "hot" neighborhood.

Most of the participants in this process tend to be young single persons or childless couples. One study indicated that more than half were between the ages of twenty-five and thirty-five. They tend to be middle-class or more affluent people, many of them professionals. They are well educated. A study of residents in the Hill District in St. Paul, Minnesota, indicated that 80 percent of the adults had graduated from college.[6] Many households include two wage earners taking advantage of the growth of managerial and professional jobs in central cities (26 percent rise between 1960 and 1970).

The rate of gentrification appears to be speeding up. Experts used to speak of turning around a neighborhood in five to ten years. Now it appears to be happening in some neighborhoods in less than two years.

Gentrification differs markedly from the massive urban renewal efforts of the past. It seldom involves major federally funded efforts to clear blighted areas and build large new developments or implement master plans. It is instead a largely private, often small-scale development involving small developers and individual homebuyers. It is a turnaround in the private housing market increasing in momentum until the entire neighborhood has markedly increased its economic value and changed its social and cultural composition.

As Conrad Weiler of Temple University has pointed out, however, the process has often been the result of years of massive government investment. Weiler has said:

> The present "private" reinvestment in older city neighborhoods by the middle class is the end-product of the execution of countless programs and the expenditure of billions of dollars by local, State and Federal Governments over the last 30 years all designed to stop urban blight and "save" cities, in many instances by attracting back the middle class.[7]

Gentrification is also often aided by local governments as it proceeds. In many cities, local governments—welcoming the long-awaited influx of higher income homeowners—are reinforcing the process by allocating Community Development Block Grants for improving streets, lighting, and parks and by making other rehabilitation funds available. The city of Chicago drew national attention when it floated a $100 million bond issue to make lower interest home purchase loans available to persons with net incomes as high as $60,000, a device that added substantially to middle-class interest in buying urban housing.

WHICH NEIGHBORHOODS?

Gentrification is a very selective process. The neighborhoods most likely to attract reinvestment are those close to downtown, universities, rivers, or other neighborhoods experiencing reinvestment. Another indicator of potential reinvestment is the presence of sound housing stock with architectural or historical significance (Victorian townhouses, for example). Other candidates for reinvestment are neighborhoods with strong and active neighborhood associations or community organizations. Neighborhood cohesion and organization can sometimes substitute for interesting architecture or location. These mediating structures provide the political clout, social networks, neighborhood consciousness, and sense of momentum necessary to create a favorable climate for reinvestment. Although this kind of revitalization is going on in every region, it is more likely in older, larger northern or southern cities.

Gentrification is often hailed as the answer to America's serious problems of urban decline. It is also attacked as the final blow to poor and working-class people who have seen their neighborhoods decline, only to be "rediscovered" and find themselves "gentrified out" in the process.

Actually, the process is one more tragic example of how American housing policy continues to promote neighborhoods segregated by race and income group. Just as racial steering, blockbusting, and related practices cause the resegregation of some neighborhoods, gentrification "flips" a neighborhood so that it becomes a virtually all-high-income, virtually all-white area. The economically and racially integrated community remains elusive, largely because private housing market trends promote resegregation and public policy makers either consciously reinforce those trends or fail to act effectively to mitigate their consequences.

The results of this process have therefore been mixed. The winners often include the city, which gains an expanded tax base and in some cases diverse, stronger communities with improved housing stock. Other winners include the new homeowner whose bet on the neighborhood has paid off with a new, more convenient life-style and a home rapidly appreciating in value. Still other winners are those original residents of the neighborhood who have the economic resources and tenacity to remain. They benefit from the improved public services and private businesses that frequently accompany reinvestment, and they may be able to take advantage of the acceleration in demand for housing in the area, realizing a major gain when they choose to sell their houses.

But this process produces losers as well: the long-time renter who is evicted to permit the landlord to take advantage of the new economic realities or the tenant forced out by sharp increases in rents. Another loser may be the elderly or low-income homeowner who cannot afford the rapid increases in property taxes resulting from the neighborhood's new vitality. Other losers include the homeowner who lacks knowledge or information and sells out without realizing the true value of a home or the difficulty of replacing it in today's housing market.

Revitalization in one neighborhood can cause or exacerbate problems in adjoining neighborhoods or older suburbs. The displacement of residents of Capitol Hill and other neighborhoods in Washington, D.C., is placing great pressures on Anacostia and suburban communities in Prince George's County, Maryland.

The challenge to public policy is whether new devices can be found to ensure that poor and working-class people share in the great benefits of having middle-class people move back into the city. How can we achieve balanced communities that maximize choice and allow people of different races and incomes to share in improved public schools and living conditions? How can we avoid involuntary displacement while also attracting more affluent people to the cities that need their wealth and political clout?

DISPLACEMENT

As gentrification grows, so will displacement. Over the last two or three years, displacement has become the primary concern for many community groups that a short time ago would never have dreamed their neighborhoods could attract *too much* investment. Gentrification may lead to major political and social conflict and even threaten the continued appeal of urban revitalization.

Displacement differs from normal turnover in that it is largely involuntary. It results from the eviction of tenants so that a building can be rehabilitated for higher rentals or conversion to a condominium. It results from extraordinarily rapid escalation in property taxes as an area's housing values triple or quadruple. It results also from a voluntary choice to sell a home at what appears to be a high price, often to find it resold at a much higher amount as part of spiraling speculation.

A recent report by the U.S. Department of Housing and Urban Development concluded: "We just don't know enough to estimate the national incidence of displacement with any confidence."[8] However, neighborhood and tenant groups in city after city are drawing their own conclusions from trends they see firsthand. In such cities as Portland, Maine, Oklahoma City, Louisville, and Oakland, groups are echoing the more publicized warnings of people in Washington, Boston, and San Francisco. In Conrad Weiler's words, "Reinvestment displacement exists, regardless of the state of 'data', and . . . if efforts to increase middle income innercity reinvestment are successful they will likely increase displacement."[9]

What makes displacement so disturbing is the lack of options for elderly or low-income people forced to move. They find it very difficult to find affordable housing in the same neighborhood although they want to maintain social and community ties. They run the risk of being displaced again if they are able to find housing nearby. Since revitalization is a private market phenomenon for the most part, they receive no public help in dealing with the problems of displacement.

Some turnover in urban neighborhoods is natural. We need, however, to distinguish between people being pulled out of a revitalizing neighborhood for new opportunities or to take advantage of the increased economic value of their homes and those being pushed out by eviction, higher rents, or rising taxes.

A key question is, How do the elderly, minorities, and poor and working-class families share in the "rebirth" of their neighborhoods? Combating displacement and preserving diversity have become priorities for a number of mediating structures in communities undergoing revitalization. The St. Ambrose Housing Aid Center, a counseling and real estate advocacy center in Baltimore has helped more than 700 low- and moderate-income families purchase homes in revitalizing areas.

In Detroit, the Association of Community Organizations for Reform Now (ACORN) recently waged a battle against General Motors' plans for revitalizing the low-income neighborhood just north of its world headquarters. After seriously considering moving its headquarters out of the neighborhood and perhaps out of the city, General Motors had decided instead to stay and to invest in the community. The corporation renovated its office building and adjacent buildings at a cost of $25 million and then announced a $20 million plan to rejuvenate an eighteen-block area nearby. The plans called for the purchase and renovation of 125 homes and 200 apartments, with an investment of $3.5 million in federal funds for street improvements, better lighting, and a community center.

Although the plan was backed by Mayor Coleman Young, area residents protested vehemently. With the support of ACORN's community organizers, the residents held a series of angry meetings with General Motors executives, city officials, and city councilmen. "I can understand people's concern, when they take their houses and they have no place to go," said Venola Sanders, a physical therapist whose apartment house was not bought by General Motors. "A lot of these people in these houses, they're old, they're tired, they've lived here all their lives, they don't have any place else."[10]

The community protests produced a series of important concessions. General Motors made $800,000 available for relocation expenses for people displaced by the renovation; tenants were promised a first option to live in renovated buildings; plans for subsidizing some of the housing received high priority; and General

Motors promised to give local residents preference in jobs with the corporation.

Across the nation, community organizations, churches, and other mediating structures are attempting to enlist the forces of urban revitalization in improving neighborhoods without destroying diversity or causing large-scale displacement. They are monitoring, and often opposing, the activities of government, financial institutions, and the real estate industry. They are planning and organizing to block speculators. They represent the best hope that urban revitalization will be a forerunner of broad progress in urban areas.

NEW PUBLIC POLICIES

These mediating structures, however, seldom have adequate means to channel the reinvestment process so that it benefits lower-income people and promotes diverse communities. Providing the means must become the central goal of public policy nationally and locally.

What tools would be most useful? First, since community groups and tenant organizations are the main representatives of the current residents' interests, they must be strengthened to play an effective role in combating involuntary displacement. Groups rehabilitating apartment buildings for people with lower income should receive substantial, swift support and subsidies so that they can expand their efforts. For example, Chicago's "Voice of the People" in the difficult Uptown area with its shifting population, often poor and marginal, has undertaken a dynamic and effective rehabilitation program designed to assist the present population. It should receive support from governmental agencies before gentrification again drives out the poor and the elderly. The efforts of the St. Ambrose Housing Aid Center in Baltimore, which is as successful a counseling and rehabilitation effort as exists in the country, with many years of experience, should receive help for added staff and be duplicated in other cities across the land as quickly as possible. Tenant organizations seeking to purchase buildings for current residents—like Washington's church-based group called Jubilee Housing—should receive substantial backing from public sources. Groups taking tough stands to promote controls on speculation, condominium conversion, and the like should be given high priority for funding by church and other philanthropic sources.

Second, city governments should quickly redirect their Community Development Block Grant (Section 8, Section 312) and other programs to promote the interests of current residents in gentrifying areas. High priority should be given to rehabilitating housing for current residents by making public grants and loans to people with limited incomes and by devising programs that encourage apartment owners to renovate buildings while controlling rents so that elderly and other lower income people can benefit.

Third, city governments should devise new ways of ensuring that tax, zoning, code enforcement, and building permit policies are geared to the needs of current residents in gentrifying areas. There should be serious attempts to keep property taxes from skyrocketing as property values escalate—such as postponement of major increases until a house is sold, restriction on the speed with which taxes can increase, or a "circuit breaker" exempting elderly and lower income people from tax increases.

Fourth, city governments should introduce controls on condominium conversion, taxes on speculation, and plans to spread out reinvestment. Washington, D.C., now requires that 51 percent of the tenants in low-rent buildings consent to condominium conversion before it is permitted. The city also gives tenants a first option to purchase apartment buildings when they are offered for sale and imposes heavy taxes on people who buy and sell properties quickly for unusual profits. Other cities are searching for ways to spread out reinvestment to make sure that it is not all concentrated in a single "beachhead" where gentrification is rampant but instead leads to a broad, gradual movement of middle-class people into neighborhoods, thus promoting stable integrated communities rather than resegregation.

Although these policies must be carried out locally by city and county governments, the federal government has a major responsibility for providing leadership and resources as gentrification proceeds. Congress recognized this in 1978 when it added the following section to the Housing and Urban Development Act:

Sec. 902. The Congress declares that in the administration of Federal housing and community development programs, consistent with other program goals and objectives, involuntary displacement of persons from their homes and neighborhoods should be minimized. In furtherance of the objective stated in the preceding sentence, the Secretary of Housing and Urban Development shall conduct a study on the nature and extent of such displacement, and, not later than January 31, 1979, shall report to the Congress on recommendations for formulation of a national policy to minimize involuntary displacement caused by the implementation of the Department's programs, and to alleviate the problems caused by displacement of residents of the Nation's cities due to residential and commerical development and housing rehabilitation, both publicly and privately financed. In carrying out such study, the Secretary shall (1) consult with representatives of affected public interest groups, government, and the development and lending industries; (2) provide data on the nature and scope of the displacement problem, both past and projected, and identify steps needed to improve the availability of such data; and (3) report fully on the current legal and regulatory powers and policies of the Department to prevent or compensate for displacement caused by its own programs.[11]

In the words of the Senate Banking and Currency Committee:

> The Committee is concerned that neighborhoods may be resegregated at the expense of the present low- and moderate-income residents, and it is for this reason that the Committee has included in Sec. 103 a requirement that the Housing Assistance Plan of each locality include specific programs to provide displaced residents with opportunities to relocate within their neighborhoods, and to ensure that existing residents benefit from neighborhood revitalization.[12]

These statements of principle are, in themselves, of little effect. They point, however, to a growing national concern with displacement and the beginning of a search for means to channel reinvestment so that it benefits lower-income people.

REFERENCES

1. Thomas J. Black, "Private Market Housing Renovation in Central Cities," *Urban Land* (November 1975): 3–9.
2. Nathaniel H. Rogg, *Urban Housing Rehabilitation in the United States* (United States League of Savings and Loan Associations, 1977), p. 9.
3. Franklin James, Testimony before Housing Banking Committee (U.S. House of Representatives, July 8, 1977).
4. Phillip L. Clay, "Neighborhood Revitalization: The Recent Experience in Large American Cities," unpublished manuscript, (MIT, 1978).
5. Rolf Goetze, Kent Colton, and Vincent O'Donnell, *Stabilizing Neighborhoods* HUD contract 191977 (Department of Housing and Urban Development, November 1977).
6. Phyllis Myers and Gordon Bender, *Neighborhood Conservation: Lessons from Three Great Cities* (Conservation Foundation, 1977).

7. Conrad Weiler, "Reinvestment Displacement: HUD's Role in a New Housing Issue," unpublished manuscript, January 1978.

8. "What's Good for General Motors May Not Be Good for Neighbors," *New York Times* (February 7, 1979).

9. Weiler, "Reinvestment Displacement."

10. U.S. Department of Housing and Urban Development, *Interim Displacement Report*—HUD–PDR–382 (Washington, D.C.: February 1979).

11. Housing and Urban Development Act of 1978, sec. 902.

12. U.S. Congress, Senate, Committee on Banking and Currency, Report No. 95–175, 95th Cong., 1st sess., 1977.

7 PUBLIC POLICY AND MEDIATING STRUCTURES

The story we have attempted to tell by looking at mediating structures in various parts of our urban areas is relatively simple. We have argued that significant numbers of people are frustrated in their attempts to secure "a decent home in a suitable environment." We have further argued that such mediating structures as neighborhood, church, family, and voluntary associations provide important resources for dealing with housing problems.

We have argued throughout that the country's housing problems are both physical and social. Just as pressing as the shortages of decent structures are the shortages of decent environments. We have seen overwhelming evidence that locational preferences are affected by the ambience and environment of a neighborhood as much as by the physical characteristics of the housing. We have attempted to show that the greatest potential for affecting this environment lies in the energies and resources of people in their primary associations.

At present, we believe, megastructures, both private and public, do not take mediating structures seriously. We do. The catch-22 is that the most important policy change imaginable would be not any single programmatic initiative but a change in attitude and sensibility. The web of affiliations between government and mediating structures is complex and entangled. It involves not only specific statutes but a variety of discretionary, administrative decisions. Hence the success of any policy based on mediating structures will depend on the outlook and sensibility of government officials at every level. As important as administrative decisions will be the public speech and symbolic moves that affect sensibilities.

We have attempted in what follows to balance broad objectives and specific programs. Sometimes we have presented concrete proposals, but our aim is not to present a ready-made legislative agenda. Individual proposals would need to be examined in more detail than appears here. Rather we attempt to show what public policy would look like if one took mediating structures seriously. We believe a policy based on the *logic* of these proposals would aid citizens in their attempts to fashion better lives.

We have made two general assumptions. The first is that certain needs must be addressed by the national government. Particularly, we think long-term improvement in housing will depend to a major degree on economic and employment advancement. Nothing said here should detract from the urgency of economic advancement of the poor. Mediating structures can aid in this process, but our primary task is to concentrate on housing. Second, we have assumed that national government resources will continue to be limited for the foreseeable future. We do propose some budgetary increases but in general have attempted to identify programs that lever and energize existing resources of mediating structures.

Our proposals are grouped under seven principles:
1. Public investment in housing
2. Elimination of anti–mediating structures policies by government
3. Elimination of triage
4. Redistribution of resources to low- and middle-income neighborhoods
5. Enhancement of the role of mediating structures in housing policy
6. Greater enforcement of civil rights laws
7. Greater balance between private megastructures and mediating structures

PUBLIC INVESTMENT IN HOUSING

The goal of "a decent home for every American" seemed within reach for a decade but that goal has become a mirage. The United States is now suffering a net loss of rental housing each year as abandonment wipes out low-income rental housing and condominium conversion reduces the middle-income stock. At the same time, inflation is making the dream of homeownership increasingly illusory.

Government is pulling back from its historical commitment to housing. Over the last decade it has reduced the number of new housing units it subsidizes each year by 60 percent, and further reductions are planned. The Department of Housing and Urban Development (HUD) has done little to respond to the major housing problems discussed in this book—redlining, speculation, displacement, discriminatory real estate practices, and abandonment— through studies, regulation, or new programs. HUD is strikingly isolated from these problems and from the efforts of people's organizations to address them.

One reason for this has been HUD's perception of its constituency. In the words of the National Commission on Neighborhoods:

> Thus, lenders, developers, and local governments are able to shape HUD's policies all the way from the legislative stage of implementation and daily working procedures. One can understand how, under their influence, it is easy for HUD to confuse these lenders, developers and local government officials with its actual clients.[1]

The federal government administers several programs designed to improve housing conditions for lower income people. These include the Section 8, Section 515, and public housing programs to provide rental housing at reduced cost, and, for rural areas, the Section 502 program to reduce the costs of homeownership. Each has its defenders and its detractors, and all suffer from declining federal support, slow, complicated procedures, and weak public support— since the public is only dimly aware of these programs and what they can accomplish.

The programs were not designed to reinforce or assist mediating structures. In fact, the public housing and other rental programs have largely ignored the interests and potentially valuable roles of tenant organizations, and none of the programs lends itself well to initiative, sponsorship, or even input by community groups or voluntary associations. The various programs, in fact, have been largely dominated by the megastructures.

New Directions in Housing Policy

There is unquestionably a need for a massive increase in the public resources devoted to helping people obtain decent housing. These resources could increase incomes by creating jobs, provide an overall income supplement for those with low incomes, supplement people's ability to cover shelter costs through a housing allowance, or reduce housing costs through subsidies.

We have no specific amount of increase in mind and do not propose to balance housing needs against others in the competition for public financial resources. But it must be made clear that more resources are needed to solve the housing problems of the nation.

We can address the question of the desirable directions of new policies and propose certain basic principles we believe must be central to future housing policy. First, housing policy must no longer be left to the technicians, politicians, and vested interests. There must be a major campaign to alert the public to alarming new housing trends and the need for broad-scale debate concerning the best ways to address and cope with new issues.

Public debate and public education are essential if people are to understand and support the measures that will ensure decent housing in the future. The nation cannot afford to leave its housing policies obscure and unresponsive to current needs.

Second, housing as well as job/income approaches must be made more cost-effective. Costs would be reduced, the impact of housing programs on the budget made more visible, and government fiscal accountability increased by shifting to programs that rely on capital grants rather than loans. This would mean relying on the Treasury rather than banks, on fees rathers than tax shelters, and on non-profit or local public agency sponsorship rather than on profit-making initiatives.

Third, the interests and potential of mediating structures should be taken into account in the design and implementation of any new housing programs. Community groups, tenant groups, and voluntary associations have much to offer in improving housing—in site selection, building design appropriate for the tenants and the neighborhood, management and maintenance, counseling tenants or homebuyers, and participating directly in the development and construction. Thus far they have had to try to bend megastructure-dominated programs to their needs. New programs should be structured to offer them a substantial role in setting policy for future housing projects and a direct role in development where appropriate. Federal agencies should also offer them financial and technical assistance and cooperation.

Fourth, to ensure that the megastructures no longer distort ongoing programs and that HUD begins to see housing consumers and neighborhood groups as key clients, the department should create panels of tough, independent, and informed citizens to conduct six-month assessments of the impact of each HUD program on local housing. These panels should have independent staffs, full access to information available within HUD, and a mandate to recommend new policies that would respect the interests of local citizens and consumers.

Fifth, there should be careful exploration of the possibility of a federal housing block grant program. Like the Community Development Block Grant (CDBG), a housing block grant could decentralize decision making to the local level and create flexibility for creative approaches to meeting the enormously varied needs of different communities. Designed properly with citizen participation and run well, this could be a great advance. But designed with inadequate safeguards and insufficient attention to either a serious citywide effort among local governments or a major role for mediating structures, a housing block grant program could suffer from the same faults as CDBG.

To be useful, a housing block grant program would need to be designed to enforce civil rights laws. It would also need provisions for monitoring and evaluation by independent citizen groups empowered to challenge any failures by the local government to meet federal standards or to respond to neighborhood needs. Finally, it would need provisions allowing the federal government to bypass any local government that fails to meet these standards and to provide direct funding to mediating structures where feasible.

ELIMINATION OF ANTI-MEDIATING
STRUCTURES POLICIES BY GOVERNMENT

Eliminating anti-mediating structures policies involves such general issues as taxation, family policy, and welfare. If mediating structures are to be strengthened in the area of housing, they must be strengthened in general. Our focus here, however, will be on ways in which government policy negatively affects these structures in housing matters.

Our case studies have revealed a number of past and present practices that severely damaged mediating structures. Urban renewal's indiscriminate razing and the practice of redlining by the Federal Housing Administration (FHA) stand as two prime examples. Such practices continue, and they sap the strength of mediating structures.

Perhaps the most serious abuse comes when government action, directly or indirectly, is damaging to existing neighborhoods. One major example is triage, letting "mortally wounded" or "unviable" neighborhoods die. As shown in the chapters on transition and suburban areas, this policy causes migration from doomed areas and places great pressures on "second-tier" neighborhoods. Triage will be more fully discussed below.

The whole argument for mediating structures is that primary worlds of meaning are experienced locally through church, family, neighborhood, and voluntary associations. Some changes come as a result of unalterable forces. Others result from government decisions, such as those affecting transportation planning, dispersal strategies, and zoning. Our general recommendation is that government minimize the amount of disruptive change introduced into neighborhoods and that government particularly avoid pushing disruptive change into second-tier and transitional neighborhoods, those least able to withstand the pressures. In particular, we think certain specific elements should be examined to minimize stress on fragile neighborhoods:

- Zoning. Localities should reexamine their zoning policies with an eye especially to the effect of proposed changes on neighborhood viability. Three zoning changes particularly destructive to neighborhoods are commercial intrusion, multifamily housing, and adult entertainment facilities in commercial areas. Practice varies from locale to locale, but on the whole local governments have tended to allow these changes in lower economic areas. In many cases, introduction of land use changes has been the final, tipping weight in an already precarious situation.

- Transportation. Both locally and nationally, an increased role should be given to neighborhoods in decision making about physical disruption of urban areas.
- Urban renewal. Although the promising days of urban renewal are over, some cities are experiencing commercial revitalization. Governments should strengthen participation mechanisms to guard against destruction similar to that of the 1950s and 1960s.
- Public housing. Later we make suggestions on changing the character of public housing by involving mediating structures. To the extent that traditional public housing is to be built, government should pay particular attention to location, especially in stable but fragile areas. A significantly greater role should be given to mediating structures in the planning and management of public housing. Public housing can work, but as some of our cases indicated, the support of mediating structures is crucial.
- Busing and education. The evidence seems clear that busing schoolchildren to achieve racial balance has increased white flight from the city. The irony of busing parallels the irony of the general pattern of social change in our cities and towns. Busing is presently judicially limited to intradistrict plans. In most urban areas, the districts tend to correspond with city boundaries. The affluent flee over city and school district boundaries and resegregate in suburban areas. Busing is then directed at those who have stayed in the city, whether by choice or by necessity.

A separate volume, of course, could be written on busing, but given the dramatic character of the issue, we must address it. In the context of housing policy, busing should be avoided whenever possible. Of course, educational alternatives open to all must be encouraged, but government should reexamine strategies aimed at imposing quotas or percentages and examine them in partnership with mediating structures.

To implement recommendations like those just listed is difficult. Many of the issues mentioned involve administrative decisions at many levels of government. Different mechanisms would be required at different levels. We do offer two concrete suggestions.

First, assign to the Office of Management and Budget (OMB) review power of federal agency impact on urban areas, as proposed in President Carter's urban review process. The proposal would require each federal agency to submit a statement on its programs' effect on urban areas. The OMB would then be in a position to review the cumulative effect of government's urban activities. We propose as one component of the review a specific section on neighborhood impact. This would not guarantee any outcome, but it would force decision makers to take responsibility for policies affecting the viability of neighborhoods.

Second, we suggest that HUD institute an additional requirement for Community Development Block Grant applications: that localities prepare a neighborhood impact statement in connection with decisions in zoning, education, transportation, housing, and urban renewal.

Neither of these processes would involve regulatory power directly. Their effect would be significant only as a modification in process. To strengthen the role of mediating structures, a small program of technical assistance grants should be available to help neighborhood groups, associations, and churches prepare rebuttals and supply additional information after reviewing both federal and local neighborhood impact statements. This is, in fact, what such structures do best, that is, mediate between individuals and larger institutions. These proposals would modestly improve the expertise of mediating structures in the process of mediation.

ELIMINATION OF TRIAGE

Triage, the policy of allowing the mortally wounded to die while devoting scarce resources to viable patients, looks all too attractive to decision makers at every level. In practice it may be called by different names, such as leverage, targeting, or selective intervention. The neighborhoods may be identified as unviable, inner city, poor, or obsolete. Anthony Downs, in his influential book *Opening Up the Suburbs,* summarizes the assumptions of the policy: "Most urban neighborhoods containing relatively high concentrations of low income households are neither economically nor socially viable."[2]

Downs says that "relatively high concentrations" can exist "even when far less than half of its occupants have incomes below the official poverty line." He argues that resources should not be wasted on attempting to transform these "crisis ghettoes." At the same time, their people should be channeled away from the fragile second-tier neighborhoods. Downs concludes that residents of these areas should be dispersed in suburban areas through large-scale public housing subsidies, located in such a way as to preserve the present economic, social, and cultural dominance in the suburban areas. Downs's book, published in 1973, has been an important influence on policy makers. It is our belief that essentially one-third of his proposal has been adopted—that of withdrawing resources from the poorest neighborhoods. At the same time that HUD, for example, has begun to caution cities against putting funds into non-viable areas, the amount of the subsidized public housing in suburban areas has increased only negligibly.

Triage has one particularly serious drawback. It probably will not work. The dispersal strategy assumes that poor people in bad neighborhoods will be better off in middle-income and upper income areas, brought there by such means as busing, forced or induced acceptance of public housing or quotas. One fundamental reason why this will not work is that present laws and judicial interpretations have made massive dispersal almost impossible. The *Arlington* and *Detroit School* court cases have eliminated for all practical purposes forced busing across school district lines and have ruled that zoning in suburbs cannot be considered discriminatory unless plaintiffs can prove *intent* to exclude on racial grounds. Given this and federal government's present inactivity in building public housing, the prospects for racial and economic dispersal across political boundaries are zero.

Dispersal *within* city and school district boundaries is the actual alternative, and we believe this is disastrous to lower-middle- and middle-income areas. Further, we have argued that it is devastating to the poorest people. The Morris Park experience, for example, shows the plight of those left behind in the poorest neighborhoods.

Perhaps most important, a mediating structures approach recognizes that many residents of poor areas wish to remain and to improve their neighborhoods. The case study of Morris Park and other transitional areas indicates the positive role mediating structures can play in rejuvenating severely blighted areas. We are not proposing that the poor be forced to live in ghetto areas by deliberately denying them opportunities to move. Even as some people want to remain in their neighborhoods, others want to leave. We will argue later that dispersal into suburban areas should be implemented with the aid of mediating structures, a possibility the triage-dispersal theorists almost completely ignore. Our point here is that massive dispersal is, at present, an illusion and that over the next five to eight years the denial of resources to so-called unviable neighborhoods will worsen the situation for everyone. The poor will only see their neighborhood deteriorate further, as private funds vanish along with public.

We do not deny that *some* areas are not viable, but experience suggests that they are relatively rare; that is, few areas are so bad that the only thing to do is tear them down and send all the residents packing. We have been impressed time and again with the desire of at least some residents in most areas to defend and revitalize their neighborhood.

Rather than bureaucratically deciding that a neighborhood is unviable, government should be more responsive to groups' attempts to rejuvenate their areas. In Chicago the city declared a small Lithuanian neighborhood "severely blighted" and planned to demolish all structures and sell the land for parking. An outcry arose, surveys were taken, and it was discovered that the vast majority of residences were in good condition and that the area had a relatively small incidence of poverty, a moderate crime rate, and, most important, an intense sense of community. Even though they were offered relocation payments, the people objected to their neighborhood's being destroyed, and most opted to stay.

The South Bronx is another example. In many ways, it presents the worst images of urban America. Do planners seriously propose to relocate 700,000 residents in the near future? If not, do they suggest telling the residents that their neighborhood is wholly unviable? Do they suggest that church and neighborhood groups successfully rehabilitating buildings close up shop?

We suggest that both HUD and local areas adopt a process of formal public hearings with citizen participation before declaring areas irreversibly "blighted." We further recommend that HUD and local agencies reexamine the assumption that poor areas are unviable. Revitalization has failed in part because it has neglected mediating structures. Resources can be profitably directed to areas where mediating structures are committed to renewal.

REDISTRIBUTION OF RESOURCES TO
LOW- AND MIDDLE-INCOME NEIGHBORHOODS

Serious efforts to come to the aid of the least advantaged entail
increasing the resources available. At present older lower middle-
income and lower income neighborhoods are probably receiving
less than their proportional share of Community Development
Block Grant (CDBG) funds. Nathan's study indicated that this
was true of revenue sharing. HUD is conducting a major study of
the CDBG program, and there is evidence to suggest that the pattern
will emerge with clarity. To reject triage means to embrace the
notion that, if people desire, poor neighborhoods can be made
decent and viable. But that necessitates providing adequate resources
to do the job. In other times we might have suggested an additional
$5 billion in special block grants for these neighborhoods; but
although we make some budgetary recommendations later, we
concentrate here on the reallocation of existing resources. We recommend that statutory guidelines be established allocating minimum
percentages of CDBG funds for low- and moderate-income neighborhoods. A similar regulation, administratively promulgated in
1978, was emasculated by an amendment in Congress later that
year. Mayors strenuously objected to the regulation. Two reasons
seemed to prompt their opposition to targeting. First, mayors find
discretionary funds their greatest political asset. Second, many
mayors and their planning staffs have wholeheartedly adopted
the triage concept and argue that investment in low-income areas
is throwing money away. We have attempted to show the possibilities of revitalization on a local level, employing the leadership
of mediating structures. Mayors and planners must begin to examine
these possibilities instead of rejecting them on limited political
grounds.

ENHANCEMENT OF THE ROLE OF MEDIATING
STRUCTURES IN HOUSING POLICY

Proposals presented here are tentative. Not every program can be
designed to suit every neighborhood or group. The effectiveness
of any particular program depends on the stability and strength
of the neighborhood and the associations involved. What follows

is a graduated series of suggestions, ranging from mild to intense involvement of mediating structures.

Facilitation of Private Funding

In conducting forty case studies of neighborhood organizations, the National Commission on Neighborhoods found that approximately 80 percent of the organizations had raised funds locally through membership dues, special events, and contributions. These sources, however, usually become a relatively small part of the budgets as the organizations grow.

Such sources of funds as the Ford Foundation, the Campaign for Human Development of the Roman Catholic Church, and other church groups and foundations have played a critical role in providing "no strings" support for the operations of community organizations involved in housing issues and other social issues and projects. Local mediating structures have generally found it healthier to receive funds from several sources that allow their grants to cover staff costs. This "core funding" provides the flexibility community groups need to be responsive to shifting neighborhood concerns and to new issues and projects.

Unfortunately, private support is scarce. Relatively few of the nation's philanthropic foundations have provided funding for neighborhood groups, tenant organizations, or voluntary associations working on housing problems. For example, virtually none of the 1,600 foundations in Los Angeles County provides any support for such activities. Most foundations prefer to fund "safe" or noncontroversial groups. Year after year promising local groups find themselves devoting enormous amounts of their time to fund raising.

Local and national churches have made very valuable contributions, but these sources are also limited. More than 70 percent of the neighborhood groups surveyed by the National Commission on Neighborhoods received their earliest outside support from churches, but the commission found church bodies deeply concerned about the shortage of funding agencies willing to pick up the burden of continuing support after seed money is spent. The problem has been aggravated in recent years as such historically important sources as the Fund for the Self-Development of Peoples of the United Presbyterian Church and the development fund of the National

Council of Churches have found themselves with few dollars to invest in community groups.

The United Way and corporations, with few exceptions, have been of little help to mediating structures. In a recent report on private funding for neighborhood organizations, the National Committee for Responsive Philanthrophy concluded that such donors tend to be ignorant of and insensitive to neighborhood groups.

Private donors are often simply unaware of the roles mediating structures are playing in neighborhoods with housing problems. Living in communities where housing is not a problem, socializing with people of similar income and class background who are not involved with neighborhood and tenant organizations, and familiar only with the needs of traditional charities, many donors simply do not understand the importance of support for such groups. Furthermore, since leaders of such groups are not part of the "old boy network," they lack the informal access to donors so often crucial in obtaining private support.

A number of policy changes would increase private support for mediating structures. First, changes in the federal income tax treatment of charitable contributions could increase individual giving. Two revisions would be especially helpful. The first would allow all taxpayers to itemize and deduct their charitable contributions, whether or not they use the standard deduction. Some 77 percent of all taxpayers now use the standard deduction and do not itemize charitable contributions. Therefore, 77 percent of the American people currently have no tax incentive to make charitable contributions. Allowing all taxpayers to itemize and deduct their charitable contributions should greatly increase individual giving.

Similarly, allowing people to take a tax credit rather than a deduction for charitable contributions would give people of low and middle incomes an incentive to help. Those in relatively low income tax brackets now receive less of a tax break for charitable contributions than those in higher income tax brackets. A shift from a deduction to a tax credit or to a system that allows a taxpayer to choose whichever approach is more beneficial would increase charitable giving by the less affluent.

The National Committee on Responsive Philanthrophy emphasizes the importance of opening up decision making within private foundations, the United Way, and corporate donors. The committee stresses that such openness will increase accountability and promote greater communication between donors and potential applicants for funds.

Changes within United Way agencies could increase funding for neighborhood organizations. The Milwaukee United Way, for example, has experimented with a special allocations committee to review funding requests related to neighborhood needs. Other United Way agencies are changing their procedures for donations at the workplace, so that employees may contribute to the charity of their choice, not just to United Way members. Since very few community groups have been admitted as members of United Way and therefore very few have access to the payroll deduction system, such an opening of workplace solicitation could bring great benefits to mediating structures.

These and other changes in private and public policies could provide crucially important support for housing groups. They deserve serious attention from Congress, the executive branch, and leaders of private philanthropies.

Neighborhood Housing Services Model

One of the most promising programs sponsored by government and one of the few involving mediating structures directly is the Neighborhood Housing Services (NHS) of the Federal Home Loan Bank Board. Described in Chapter 2, NHS gives grants to local consortiums made up of financial institutions, local governments, and neighborhood associations in target areas. The federal government provides start-up money and subsidizes staff operations. Financial institutions agree to make mortgage and rehabilitation loans in the target area. Neighborhood associations provide counseling and referral to residents. City government commits itself to certain improvements as well as a comprehensive code inspection and enforcement. Participants from all three sectors have found the experience fruitful in improving housing quality and demand for housing in designated areas.

Programs like this are natural beginnings to a mediating structures policy. Churches and voluntary associations may eventually play larger roles, but in most areas the mediating structures need to develop capacity over a period of time before moving into larger projects. In the NHS concept, they do what they do best—mediate between the residents and the municipal and financial institutions. Cities find, for example, that the support of a church or community organization is invaluable in systematic code enforcement. Only an institution with the direct loyalty of the residents can blunt the fears associated with inspection and enforcement. NHS funding should be provided to a larger number of cities and neighborhoods within cities. (At present only one neighborhood per city is allowed in the program.) An orderly but substantial enlargement could be accomplished with an additional $75 million per year. One advantage of this program is that it does not involve large-scale federal grants or subsidies. The federal money is used to energize and balance private and municipal and neighborhood resources.

HUD and the NHS Concept

HUD should expand the NHS concept by instituting a wider variety of programs involving grants to neighborhood organizations, churches, and voluntary associations. At present NHS funding concentrates on counseling and referral. Mediating structures are the local entities to perform such activities, as exemplified by the Oak Park Housing Organization in its successful handling of integration. If HUD were to concentrate on the bottom half of neighborhoods in the country, this would involve about 5,000 grants. Over a three-year period, HUD could give each neighborhood $50,000 per year with about 1 percent of its annual budget.

Three components of such a program would require attention. First, what activities should be eligible? The range of activities should be relatively large but *specified*. One problem of the Model Cities program was the absence of limits on eligible activities. We would propose a specified list of activities, such as counseling, office maintenance, communication with residents, tool banks, beautification, painting supplies, rehabilitation, land acquisition, anticrime programs, education programs, job training and counseling, insulation, and winterization. Under this program, emphasis should be on activities that mediating structures do best and programs that would simultaneously help them develop capacity for other tasks.

Second, how much to devote to the program? Minuscule amounts (relative to the entire HUD and Community Services Administration (CSA) budgets) are now available for counseling and neighborhood projects. Initially each neighborhood below the sixtieth percentile in income should receive a grant annually during a three-year cycle. This would cost about $150 million per year. Performance could be evaluated during the period, with further funding depending on performance.

Third, who is eligible? Increasingly this question is becoming less acute because of the upsurge in neighborhood-based activity. In a sample of sixty American cities conducted by the University of Notre Dame, fifty-seven had defined or were in the process of defining their neighborhoods. More than half had completed the task or had timetables for doing so. Interviews in all sixty cities indicated that problems over boundaries were relatively minor and could be resolved. In most cases, it was reported that conflicts between groups were not a serious problem in involving the neighborhood in policy. Hence one alternative is simply to let any representative mediating structure apply, be it church, community organization, neighborhood group, or other voluntary association. If and when conflicts over representation occur, an appeals process could be instituted involving HUD local officials and members of neighborhood organizations.

Our proposal differs significantly from the Model Cities program in four respects: it is open to all lower income and middle-income neighborhoods; it comes at a different time in history; it does not attempt to create a representative structure, but rather responds to indigenous structures (a church, for example, could be the representative); and it would include legislative standards on eligible activities.

HUD should encourage local variants of this process by providing a pool of matching funds as an add-on to CDBG funds. HUD would match, up to a limit, funds localities allocated for direct grants to churches and neighborhood groups in neighborhoods of lower and middle income.

Elimination of Obstacles to Funding of Mediating Structures

There has been a long and bitter battle at the national level over funding of neighborhood groups. Local officials have strongly opposed such programs since the days of the "War on Poverty," when some federally funded community action agencies took tough advocacy positions on behalf of the poor and minorities, much to the consternation of local officials and some members of Congress.

The U.S. Conference of Mayors opposes direct funding of community groups.

As a result of this opposition, there are currently few federal programs to provide either core support or project funding for community groups, and those programs are controversial. HUD's new Office of Neighborhood Development (OND), for example, has had to fight a hard battle inside HUD and in Congress for enactment of a program to provide a mere $10 million a year to neighborhood development organizations. It has had to accept a bar on funding for groups not endorsed by local mayors—an onerous limitation in places as diverse as Chicago, Illinois, and Jackson, Mississippi—and to limit its program to single specific projects rather than core support. Similarly, when ACTION proposed a Good Neighbor Fund providing grants of $5,000 to $15,000 for neighborhood projects, that agency also had to agree to mayoral concurrence.

A few federal programs provide direct funding for community groups without mayoral approval, but these are rare. As a result, in cities like Cleveland, where the mayor was opposed to funding for any neighborhood groups, the development of mediating structures was held back by political considerations. The veto or concurrence requirement gives mayors an effective monopoly over federal funding for neighborhood preservation efforts and constitutes a direct threat to the pluralism and emphasis on voluntary associations that have characterized the United States since its birth.

All policies and procedures that give local officials, in effect, a veto over federal funding, training, or technical assistance for mediating structures should be eliminated. Instead, local officials should be given thirty days within which to review and comment on proposals from community organizations. Those comments should be considered on their merits by federal officials reviewing the proposals, with special concern for compatibility with local government's plans and priorities. Negative comments should not constitute a veto, any more than citizen complaints against CDBG or other federal programs run by local governments should lead to automatic disapproval.

At the same time, the various block grant, revenue sharing, and categorical programs that provide federal funds to local governments should be opened to community groups.

Technical Assistance

Access to adequate technical assistance is equally important. Mediating structures desperately need information, advice, and assistance from people experienced in local program areas. They need information about what works and what does not, where to go for help, and what new trends should be considered as they develop their programs. They need access to lawyers, financial analysts, government experts, management specialists, and others.

Several foundations have recognized the importance of technical assistance and have given support to private, nonprofit technical assistance organizations. Foremost among these have been the Ford Foundation and the Charles Stewart Mott Foundation. On the whole, however, relatively little philanthropic money has gone to technical assistance organizations.

There has been greater support for technical assistance from various federal programs, including those administered by HUD's Office of Neighborhood Development, the Neighborhood Reinvestment Commission (which has its own in-house technical assistance capacity), and the Office of Community Anti-Crime Programs of the Law Enforcement Assistance Administration.

There has been considerable controversy over federal funding for private, nonprofit technical assistance organizations, paralleling the debate over direct federal funding for community groups. The legislation authorizing appropriations for OND, for example, allows mayors to veto the delivery of any technical assistance to community groups. This restriction even bars invitations to representatives of neighborhood groups to OND-funded training sessions without the approval of local officials. There was a similar battle over technical assistance to neighborhood groups under the Community Development Block Grant program, with mediating structures eventually losing the argument that federal regulations give them the right to choose their own technical advisers.

Neighborhood groups and federal agencies agree that the key to successful self-help programs can often be access to advice and assistance from outside specialists. It is therefore important that Congress remove its current restrictions on technical assistance delivery. Federal agencies should review their policies with the objective of increasing the support available to community groups for consultants of their own choice.

Access to Information

Community groups often find themselves unable to gain access to essential information about public and private policies that have an impact on their neighborhoods. Until the Home Mortgage Disclosure Act was enacted in 1975, for example, community groups found it difficult to study disinvestment in their neighborhoods. In cities like Chicago, it is virtually impossible for tenants, church groups, or others to learn the names of the owners of apartment buildings held in blind trusts. Groups attempting to monitor the expenditure of CDBG or other federal funds often themselves denied access to documents that show who—by race, income group, and neighborhood—is benefiting from housing rehabilitation or job creation programs. There is a serious need for measures to increase access to such information.

First, the federal Freedom of Information Act should be extended to require local and state governments to respond to inquiries for information about locally administered federal programs. Just as federal programs have been decentralized, the responsibility of operating them in an open and accountable manner must also be decentralized. In the housing context, it is especially important that freedom of information requirements be extended to local governments administering the $4 billion CDBG program.

Second, for similar reasons "sunshine" requirements should be introduced for all federal programs administered by local governments. All meetings in which decisions are made on the allocation of public funds or on public policies with regard to housing and CDBG programs should be open to the public and announced in advance.

Third, the lessons of the Home Mortgage Disclosure Act should be applied to other areas of private institutional behavior. Without red tape or substantial cost, the disclosure act has made extraordinarily important information available to individuals and groups concerned with housing investment patterns. It has thus enabled those groups to document and tackle redlining problems. Also beneficial are the Federal Home Loan Bank Board's new requirement that savings and loans associations develop written loan-underwriting standards and the Community Reinvestment Act's requirement that lenders publish a map and a statement showing where they will make loans. A disclosure approach should be extended to property ownership, at least of multifamily buildings, and to insurance companies, requiring them to indicate where they do and do not insure homes and automobiles.

Lobbying

There is a serious inequity in the treatment of the political and advocacy efforts of mediating structures compared with those of private megastructures. Banks, real estate firms, and developers seeking to influence legislation or administrative action can deduct their costs from taxes and charge the expenses to their customers.

Mediating structures involved in the political or legislative process do so at some risk of losing their tax-exempt status because of Internal Revenue Code limitations on lobbying by tax-exempt charitable organizations. These restrictions should be removed so that mediating structures can become fully involved in debate on housing policy and neighborhood-related issues.

Rehabilitation Loans

HUD should provide incentives for local governments and financial institutions to make rehabilitation loans available in all areas. Some progress has been made in the fight against redlining, but the private sector version of triage continues in many areas. If mediating structures are able to increase activities in older areas, lower interest loans will be needed for residents willing to invest in those neighborhoods. An expanded NHS could fulfill this function, as could an expanded Urban Co-op Bank.

Section 8 Housing

Voluntary associations and churches should be made eligible for the development, management, and rehabilitation of Section 8 housing. At present, Section 8 is the largest housing item in the HUD budget. Except for a few demonstration grants, development is entirely in the hands of the private commercial sector. Section 8 involves construction or rehabilitation of units, the government providing rent subsidies to a certain percentage of tenants.

At present churches and community groups cannot compete for Section 8 housing. As shown in previous chapters, voluntary associations can play a vital role in bringing such housing in line with the needs and aspirations of both neighborhood residents and tenants. This program would be similar to the old 221-D-3 program, phased out in 1973, which had many successes. Its failures were generally in the area of construction and financing expertise. The main reason for its demise was the lack of technical know-how on the part of some nonprofit sponsors. In our estimation, the program was evaluated on the wrong grounds.

We would propose that nonprofit sponsors be allowed to hire technical expertise, with seed money provided by HUD. This is being done with much success under the housing programs for the elderly and for handicapped persons. The point of involving mediating structures is not to get the most efficient or expert construction management. They clearly cannot compete with professional developers. It was this implicit comparison that led to the demise of 221-D-3. The aim, from our perspective, is to draw upon the human and moral resources of the mediating structures. In the South Bronx, for example, eight rehabilitated buildings in the area nearest Manhattan are managed by the church-based South Bronx Coalition. So far the buildings are fully occupied, and vandalism is at a minimum. A successful program would provide community organizations with the funds to hire expert management skills. It would also provide government-guaranteed mortgages. In residential neighborhoods in smaller cities, the potential is especially good. A program combining start-up grants with government-insured mortgages would allow community organizations to replace the slum landlord in determining the condition of housing stock.

Regulations Concerning Public Housing Management

Regulations concerning public housing should be changed to allow and encourage the management of public housing by community groups, churches, and other voluntary associations. This would require change in the federal statute, as well as changes in local ordinances governing local housing authorities.

Abandoned Buildings

HUD and city officials should develop an aggressive policy of fore-closing on abandoned buildings, turning them over to community groups for rehabilitation and management. HUD has done this with single-family FHA and VA homes under its homesteading program. HUD should fund programs to allow city community development programs to develop speedier foreclosure procedures in abandonment and tax delinquency cases in multifamily housing and pay community groups to rehabilitate and manage them. Local officials should devote some of their CDBG funds for development of such programs. Examples such as Morris Park indicate how relatively small resources can positively affect the capacity of voluntary associations to conserve housing stock. Our argument is that the only alternative is demolition. Case after case indicates that without the supportive network of mediating structures rehabilitation is temporary.

Volunteer Tax Credit

Congress should enact a volunteer tax credit whereby child care expenses incurred by workers in voluntary organizations qualify for a tax credit. Traditionally one spouse, whether male or female, has been the stalwart of family participation in church, voluntary association, or neighborhood organization. At present the tax code discriminates against this kind of participation. If a second spouse begins work, no matter the job or the first income, child care is deductible. We feel that if a family already making $35,000 per year can get a tax credit when the spouse starts selling golf carts, then an unpaid spouse working thirty or forty hours a week for neighborhood revitalization should qualify. This might help some families in making the choice to devote energies to local projects. More important it could serve as a positive encouragement to others who had never before been involved in their neighborhood welfare to join in and support this kind of volunteer commitment.

Modified Housing Allowance Program

A *modified* housing allowance program should be explored. The recent experiment testing the idea of a housing voucher or allowance was deemed unsuccessful because of inflation and because there was no significant increase in housing quality. Some also found it unsettling that many poor people used the greater monetary resources for things other than housing (allowed under the program). We do not find this so unsettling, since the choice should be theirs. But more unsettling were the cases where attempts were made to improve housing conditions and only higher prices resulted. From our perspective this was predictable, since nothing was done to increase either the supply of housing or the number of neighborhoods with acceptable conditions. Our analysis indicates that the present financial and real estate megastructures can always be counted on to maximize profit and minimize service.

If changes were made that allowed mediating structures to respond effectively to increased demand, the situation might be quite different. In South Bend, Indiana, for example, one of the two complete test sites, the housing allowance program was beneficial to participants in a church-run rehabilitation undertaking called RENEW. Here the church had access to development funds through the national Catholic Campaign for Human Development. RENEW bought and rehabilitated homes, and the housing allowance subsidy made it possible for tenants to make payments high enough to accumulate sufficient equity to purchase the homes after two years. Adopting a strengthened role for mediating structures in supplying housing might make the housing allowance an attractive proposition. At present, any increased demand is met only by megastructural profiteering.

Gentrification Recapture Provisions

It should be clear from the previous chapter that gentrification is a mixed blessing. In some cases it aids everyone by increasing the tax base, common interest in city services and schools, and so on. In other cases, there is total displacement of older and poorer residents and severe disruption of mediating structures. When, for example, older middle-class rental buildings in newly attractive areas are changed to condominiums, thousands of families are forced out. With them are dispersed established social and religious patterns, almost impossible to reestablish. Three measures should be explored initially:

- Condominium conversions should be subject to zoning approval. Neighborhood residents should have a strong voice on whether buildings are to be changed from rental to condominium.
- The fledgling Urban Co-op Bank, recently initiated, should be given an additional $50 million with the specific purpose of aiding indigenous residents, in both single-family and multi-family housing, to become owners in gentrified areas.
- Localities should not only direct their efforts to architecturally and historically quaint buildings but also provide incentives for young families to purchase homes in a variety of neighborhood settings.

GREATER ENFORCEMENT OF CIVIL RIGHTS LAWS

The sixth broad principle is to increase enforcement of civil rights and open housing laws at all levels. This is consistent with, and integral to, an empowerment strategy. The whole idea of upgrading poorer neighborhoods is based on the premise that substantial numbers of residents want to live in upgraded neighborhoods; the empowerment premise is that people should be able to make the decisions affecting their own lives. Some residents, under any circumstances, want to move to other areas. At present there is no question that racial discrimination prevents mobility. As indicated earlier, much of the discrimination is a confused blend of race and class discrimination. But active enforcement of existing laws can reduce the instances of pure racial discrimination. It is a plain fact that federal and local enforcement of civil rights statutes is less than optimal.

We are not talking about affirmative action. We are talking about clearly prosecutable racial discrimination. To construct a housing strategy on the idea of empowerment and then deny legal choices to individuals would be inexcusable.

GREATER BALANCE BETWEEN
PRIVATE MEGASTRUCTURES AND
MEDIATING STRUCTURES

We have given many examples of private megastructures (mortgage bankers, other financial institutions, insurance companies, real estate brokers, developers) exploiting neighborhoods and damaging mediating structures. The specifics include redlining, blockbusting, steering, exploitative foreclosure, and in some cases (as in the 235 program) outright fraud. In our contacts with neighborhood organizations and churches throughout the country, one of the most persistent demands voiced was to reduce the power these megastructures have over neighborhood life. These institutions are more powerful and more determinative of a neighborhood's future than government. The private sector controls many times more resources in housing than all federal, state, and local programs combined.

It is not our aim to indict all real estate, insurance, and financial organizations. We simply suggest that substantial abuses exist and that there are no adequate measures now on the books to deal with them.

Our central proposals are intermediate in character. That is to say, we propose a set of actions that may or may not be sufficiently long range. They should be implemented and then evaluated to determine whether stricter steps, such as regulation, should be considered.

At present there is almost no regulation of mortgage banking and real estate. Here we will concentrate especially on two practices: rapid foreclosure under insured programs and steering.

In the case of mortgage bank holdings insured by VA and FHA programs, profit is in effect guaranteed. There are relatively few incentives for the banks to insist upon accurate appraisals and no incentives for them to provide counseling to assist homeowners having difficulties in making mortgage payments. Some mortgage bankers have developed reputations for "churning" insured mortgages—sloppy appraisal and rapid foreclosure. Struggling neighborhoods can be devastated by such practices.

In real estate brokerage, major problems have been steering and blockbusting: attempts by salesmen on the one hand to steer customers away from older, integrated areas and on the other to panic owners into selling at low prices to generate quick commissions.

Our proposals essentially follow the model being developed to deal with redlining. In financial redlining, the Home Mortgage Disclosure Act requires financial institutions to make public the amount of deposits and the amount of loans by census tract. It does not mandate them to allocate credit resources to individual areas, but it allows neighborhood and church organizations to acquire the data necessary to mount an effective advocacy campaign. Since the disclosure act, there have been numerous instances in which voluntary associations have mobilized residents and brought about agreements between financial institutions and neighborhoods. We propose a mortgage banking and real estate brokerage disclosure act. Mortgage bankers would be required to release quarterly, by census tract, the number of foreclosures of residential mortgages. Real estate brokers would be required to release quarterly, by census tract, the number and aggregate dollar amount of sales they had in each area.

No individual mortgage or transaction would be revealed; so no violation of confidentiality would occur. The cost would be minimal. A large urban real estate firm might spend ten hours each quarter on the process. The advantages of such a program would be the increased ability of mediating structures to analyze patterns and devise ways of influencing the behavior of institutions. A church, for example, that suspects a particular firm of "churning" mortgages cannot now compare its foreclosure rates with those of like firms. The firm, of course, would deny such practices. Similarly in real estate, disclosure would allow mediating structures to make better judgements about which firms are acting responsibly toward the neighborhood and which are not. Would this make any difference? One way of measuring its possible effect is the amount of resistance. Real estate brokers have strenuously resisted disclosure proposals. Mortgage bankers have consistently refused to disclose voluntarily the information sought. A program of disclosure might well allow the mediating structures themselves to play a stronger role in representing the case of residents to megastructures. The alternative, of course, is allocative regulation, with government mandating allocation of resources. But this probably would not have much political appeal.

CONCLUSION

As stated before, the proposals made here would need refinement and clarification before enactment into law. But we do believe they illustrate the logic of a housing policy based on mediating structures. Although some budgetary increases are called for, the proposals certainly fall within the range of the possible.

Whether such proposals will be enacted will depend on many things. But most important, they will depend on our views of society.

Our advocacy is based on the belief that family, church, and neighborhood provide indispensable worlds of meaning and purpose to individuals and all of our society. A society with a diminished role for these elements will be quite different from a society in which they are respected and nurtured. We cannot argue, and have not attempted to do so, that mediating structures are right and effective in every case. We have argued that, on balance, they add to, rather than detract from, justice, effectiveness, and equity in housing policies. It is our firm belief that this will be even more true in the future. It is time that government fully recognizes this and begins to aid rather than harm its greatest allies in providing citizens with decent and affordable housing.

REFERENCES

1. National Commission on Neighborhood, *Final Report* (U.S. Government Printing Office, 1979), p. 14.
2. Anthony Downs, *Opening Up the Suburbs* (New Haven, Conn.: Yale University Press, 1973), p. 87.

EPILOGUE

This epilogue is addressed to the people who will make important decisions during this decade—the participants in mediating structures: the residents of neighborhoods, the members of families, churches, neighborhoods, and voluntary associations. Every significant case we have examined found the momentum for change coming from the people themselves *before* government involvement. In what follows we discuss the issues we believe must be dealt with by the mediating structures themselves if our housing problems are to be solved.

MEDIATING STRUCTURES MUST REAFFIRM THEIR OWN WORTH AND GOALS

Perhaps the greatest tragedy that could happen in the debate concerning public policy is for mediating structures to accept legitimation by the government as their chief goal. In fact their goals will, and probably should, remain in substantial tension with all levels of government. The government of the United States is and will remain a liberal one in the classic sense. The government establishes constitutional rights and rules of the game: it does not decide questions of ultimate value. Mediating structures, on the other hand,

119

are held together and given definition by shared beliefs about matters of ultimate value. Churches are obvious examples. But neighborhoods, voluntary associations, and families as well exist in that middle ground between deepest individual belief and the impersonal procedures of the state. The ability of mediating structures to bring together individuals to achieve common goals rests primarily on the network of social, cultural, and religious values extant within a community.

All too often, when they move into the area of policy, mediating structures lose their source of strength—the shared web of beliefs and values. The move becomes one of status seeking rather than achievement of the original goals. Catholic education and the battles over aid to private schools could provide some telling examples. Too often the issue is only that of government recognition of parochial schools, with the social and educational mission of the church being obscured. Similarly, voluntary associations, neighborhoods, and families run the risk of forgetting or losing their purpose and identity in the scramble for governmental recognition—and funds.

In the next decade, it is imperative for neighborhoods, families, and other mediating structures to remain faithful to their original purposes. In a liberal society, any subcommunity of shared meaning can be a prophetic presence challenging the impersonal character of the state. Neighborhood groups and community organizations will generally have to turn to government for assistance—technical or financial. But their primary commitment should be the empowerment of local residents, whether government helps or not. If people are to be empowered, the mediating structures must constantly renew their commitment to shared meanings and substantive goals.

MEDIATING STRUCTURES MUST AVOID BECOMING MEGASTRUCTURES

As interest in neighborhoods increases, there is danger that community organizations will become rigid bureaucracies similar to those controlling labor, agriculture, and professional education. One could imagine, for example, the emergence over a decade of a single large association called the National Federation of Neighborhood Groups. In the typical pattern, the national federation would develop strong alliances with congressional committees and midlevels of HUD and other bureaucracies. The federation would become part of the permanent government, and Congress and the bureaucracy would defer to it in making policy and allocation decisions. The federation would have a full-time paid staff of professionals, with dues-paying chapters in each of the states.

The national neighborhood federation approach must be measured carefully. First, political history tells us that national centralized interest groups tend to be dominated by elites. A national federation would become a megastructure. If agriculture is any example, the federation would tend to be dominated by the best-organized and most powerful interests. Policy and allocation decisions would tend to favor the most influential rather than the neediest. Professionalization would probably follow, and citizens would again find themselves in the hands of self-appointed experts.

A second and related problem is that of vitality and meaning. Mediating structures are by definition pluralistic. As stated earlier, their success in most cases depends on their ability to bring individuals together around concrete and specific issues compatible with and related to the responsibilities of the general citizenship they share. To the extent that a national bureaucracy becomes the center of decision making, the intensity and concreteness of the local group become diluted, and its greatest resources are sapped. To become a megastructure demoralizes the mediating structure and draws it away from the central purpose of empowerment.

Public policy decisions can help avoid this pitfall. For example, it appears preferable to have several smaller sources of aid in different programs for neighborhoods, rather than one large central agency controlling all funds. In this way, some of the variety and richness of the neighborhood and its people may be preserved.

But the central responsibility will rest with the members of mediating structures themselves. At present there is a marvelous diversity and disorganization to the neighborhood movement. A certain amount of coordination of mutual interest will be necessary and inevitable. But a clear-sighted resolve will be necessary to avoid the temptation to become a megastructure.

MEDIATING STRUCTURES SHOULD CONCENTRATE ON WHAT THEY DO BEST

Our policy recommendations open the possibility of greater involvement of mediating structures in the delivery of services, including, in some cases, the construction and management of housing. It should be emphasized that this will, and perhaps should, be the exception. A great danger is that churches and neighborhoods will become so involved in actual administration of programs that they lose the capacity to perform that most important function—mediating.

To the extent that a neighborhood organization, for example, becomes too enmeshed in government programs, it begins to act bureaucratically toward the residents. The main virtue of mediating structures is their ability to stand between the state and the individual and to mediate.

Housing counseling is one good example. Decisions to buy or rent, stay or flee, integrate or resegregate, are complex and emotional. Bureaucracies rarely have the care, the patience, or, most important, the credibility and trust of residents required for successful counseling in difficult situations. Churches, families, and neighborhood organizations bring precisely the kinds of qualities needed to these problems. They have the ability to relate the individual goals and aspirations and fears to a world of shared meaning and then relate those common values to the larger public or private institutions. This is the capacity policy makers should most directly stimulate, and this is the capacity mediating structures should most cherish and protect.

MEDIATING STRUCTURES SHOULD EMPOWER, NOT DOMINATE

A final point has been made repeatedly by the best observers of community and neighborhood organizations. Our own experience confirms it. The greatest temptation for leaders in a mediating structure is to begin to believe they should do things for people's best interests. What develops from such an attitude is a pernicious elitism that is self-destructive in two ways. First, it defeats the purpose of empowerment, which is to allow people individually and in groups to achieve their objectives within a constitutional and collegial framework. The whole idea of empowerment is *not* to create a situation where someone, either planner, expert, or organizer, imposes solutions on people.

Second, such an attitude is flawed in practice. Maintaining confidence in a neighborhood requires the active definition and affirmation of goals by residents. Unless the residents themselves make choices and *consequent commitments,* most neighborhood revitalization programs fail.

This is not to deny the need for the strengthening of mediating structures in staff, expertise, and leadership. But expertise and leadership must be chosen and affirmed by the people themselves and used to serve people, not vice versa.

These caveats present great challenges to the variety of groups and associations involved in grass-roots housing issues. Mediating structures must press vigorously through effective coalition building for more effective and human housing policies. At the same time, they must avoid transforming themselves into unrepresentative bureaucracies.

The American political system has many precedents for a vital and creative movement turning into a cozy oligarchic partner of the permanent government. In most cases the original sense of justice is replaced by the self-interest of organizational elites. The neighborhood movement is impressive in its richness, diversity, and local roots and values. The greatest care should be exercised to preserve those qualities.

INDEX

ABOUT THE AUTHORS

Reverend John J. Egan is director of the Center for Pastoral and Social Ministry at the University of Notre Dame.

John Carr is executive director of the White House Conference on Families.

Andrew Mott is vice-president and housing specialist at the Center for Community Change, Washington, D.C.

John Roos is associate professor of government at the University of Notre Dame and a staff member of the university's Institute for Urban Studies.